# HAMPSTEAD ONE THOUSAND

a book
to celebrate the
Hampstead Millennium
AD 986–1986

HISTORICAL PUBLICATIONS
with the London Borough of Camden

J.P.Emslie

John Richardson

# HAMPSTEAD
# ONE THOUSAND
## AD 986-1986

# ACKNOWLEDGEMENTS

In writing this book I have received much help from Malcolm Holmes, the Local History Librarian of the London Borough of Camden, and his staff. I am especially grateful, also, for the help and information given by Alan Farmer, Gerald Isaaman and Christopher Wade. Material for this book was acquired from a good many sources, but in particular I have been assisted by Roy Allen, Arthur Goss, Leslie Room, James Roose-Evans, Roy Shaw, David Sullivan and Julian Tobin.

# ILLUSTRATIONS

Except where indicated in the caption the illustrations are from the collections of either the Local History Department of the London Borough of Camden, or of the author.

The cover picture is a watercolour of St John's and Church Row by A. W. Dow in 1906.
The illustration on the title pages is of the first Long Room in Well Walk, painted by J. P. Emslie in 1879.

ISBN 0 9503656 8 8

First published 1985
Printed by Eyre and Spottiswoode at the Grosvenor Press
Typeset by Phoenix Photosetting, Chatham

Published by
Historical Publications Ltd
54 Station Road,
New Barnet, Herts.
(Telephone 01–607 1628)

In association with the London Borough of Camden

# CONTENTS

Introduction 7
1 The Whole Fragmented 9
2 The Village Centred 17
3 Expansion at the Ends 29
4 Developments in Corners 47
5 Explosion of Directions 55
6 Spaces Kept Open 71
7 Estates Divided 79
8 Traversed by Lines 95
9 Artists in their Quarters 103
10 Endeavours crossed by Wars 113
11 The whole becomes one-third 134
Appendix 1: List of Notable Residents 144
Appendix 2: List of Licensed Premises 154
Select Bibliography 155
Index 157

# Map of Hampstead 1814

By J. and W. Newton for J. J. Park, 'The topography and natural history of Hampstead'

# Introduction

It is not established that the document dated AD 986, recording a grant from Ethelred the Unready to the Abbot of Westminster of the hilltop village of Hampstead, is a forgery. If it is one, it is generally accepted that it was made for the best of reasons and only proclaimed roughly what an original document, if there had been one, would have stated. In other words, it may be a later concoction, but at least it records an actual happening. As a basis for celebrating one thousand years it therefore has some weakness, but then, there is some difficulty in coming up with the necessary paperwork for most millennium celebrations.

That particular Anglo-Saxon year was not, of course, the beginning of Hampstead or the one in which it acquired its homely name: it is merely the year of the first paper record. Recent archaeological excavations on West Heath have shown that Mesolithic men and women lived, cooked and manufactured flint implements here at least eight thousand years before Ethelred made one of his less troublesome decisions. Between these two eras there is almost a complete lack of either paperwork or unearthed remains – a Roman find or two, but nothing much which illuminates life in Hampstead.

There are also some considerable gaps in Hampstead's recorded history since Ethelred, but at least conjecture about those times has some base and comparisons to work on. From the 17th century material survives in abundance until the 19th and 20th centuries, when even a small element of Hampstead life generated enough record to provide a basis for a fat thesis with a thousand footnotes. There is now, probably, more than five times the material to distil than Thomas Barratt had to hand when he compiled his masterly three-volume *Annals of Hampstead*, published in 1912. Faced with this proliferation it is my purpose in this book to compress what I think was important in the development of the town to a manageable length.

No one invites so many sharpened pencils as he who writes a history of Hampstead: it is best to publish and disappear for a year. Omissions and interpretations will certainly be challenged and downright errors found out, for Hampstead, since the young John James Park first tested the water in 1814 with *The Topography and Natural History of Hampstead*, has always had a sufficient number of residents knowledgeable and articulate in its history to make criticism bruising and praise thoughtful.

I have used Barratt's book at times, of course, but I have tried not to repeat it or to tinker with it. F. E. Baines edited his *Records of Hampstead* in 1890, which is good for certain kinds of information but his contributors are a random bunch. E. E. Newton, a Hampstead vestryman, compiled a book which mainly recorded the activities of the old Vestry and the first ten years of the new borough council, which was formed in 1900. This is a usefully exact account, but contains not a glimmer of corporate self-reproach. Then, when Hampstead borough itself faced, with mixed feelings, a merger with its noisier neighbours to the south to form Camden, it commissioned Professor F. M. L. Thompson to write another history to bring Hampstead up to date. He concentrated on the building development of the town, eschewing rambles, artists, anecdotes and do-gooders; he combed documents unused before and produced a classic of its kind, both perceptive and witty.

Since then we have had a series of street-by-street histories edited by Christopher Wade and promoted by the Camden History Society and the High Hill Press. These publications provided a completely new fund of knowledge, especially about 20th-century residents, and they have been invaluable to me. Two publications by Christopher Ikin and Alan Farmer on the battle to save Hampstead Heath complemented Professor Thompson's account, and there have been innumerable smaller publications dealing with individual schools, churches, societies and institutions.

Especially since the last war Hampstead has been a transient town, the scene of student days for many people in various states of penury. I suspect, projecting my own feelings, that their memories of the place will be mostly fond ones. First there was the experience of independence away from family, the first serious encounters with domestic chores. Then, the freedom to arrive back to your room as late or early as you pleased to sink, without need of explanation, in front of a gas fire fed by coins, hands wrapped around a mug of instant coffee. Next, the amiable night-life, not particularly sophisticated, mainly just the film at the Everyman or the pubs where you got on with either landlord or regulars. Or the ease of Sunday mornings, complete with news-papers which made you feel already part of the great intellectual world outside, as you read them over toasted teacakes at Mr Melborne's in South End Green on one of those tables which always seemed to tilt, either because of a short leg or a sloping floor. Then there were the love affairs, of course, seemingly more blessed and intense in Hampstead, accompanied as they were by long walks on the Heath, happily in another's company, or by yourself in a state of despondency which you felt must have been the most wretched endured by anyone.

For many people, Hampstead is associated with that period of their lives. Others have lived here longer and in rather more comfort; it is they who resent most keenly the obsession with the value of real estate which has given a hard edge to Hampstead's way of life and which could ultimately destroy the urban charm which is its principal asset.

This thousandth recorded year is a good time to reflect on that.

# CHAPTER ONE

# The Whole Fragmented

Acquisitions of land in Anglo-Saxon and medieval times have shaped 19th-century development in England. Around London and near to Hampstead the Church, in some guise or other, held most of the territory; the Bishop of London had Hornsey, St Paul's had Willesden and St Pancras, and the Abbot of Westminster held Hendon and Hampstead itself. Land tenure law remained ossified so that even with the break-up of the Church holdings in the 16th century, the shapes of their estates may still be seen clearly in the pattern of 19th-century roads. The back gardens of many houses in Hampstead mark the boundaries of fields farmed by the tenants of the Norman Abbot of Westminster.

Much of England was divided into manors, areas of administration under an overlord appointed by the Crown. In Hampstead the manor was contiguous with the ecclesiastical parish and its extents may be traced in the grant of land supposedly made by the hapless Ethelred the Unready to the Abbot of Westminster in AD 986. The topographical content of that grant is as follows:

> First at Sandgate, go east to Bedegares Stynic lea; there south to Deormod's wick; from Deormod's wick to Middle Hampstead; so forth along the hay to Rushlea; from Rushlea west by the marsh to the barrow; from the barrow west along the march to Stone Grove; from the grove in to Watling Street; so north along Watling Street to Moerburn; from Moerburn again east by the march to Sandgate.[1]

Illustration 6 is an interpretation of this route put forward in 1890 by Professor John W. Hales, a noted Hampstead historian, who was much given to speculation in such matters.[2] In truth, only some of the features may be traced firmly, such as the 'barrow' (a grove south-west of Primrose Hill), and Watling Street, of course. It is reasonable to assume that Sandgate was on the sandy part of the Heath at North End, but all else in Professor Hales's map is intelligent conjecture.

Boundaries, however, were not in the habit of changing much and Professor Hales was probably near enough. Most of the eastern boundary, for example, is confirmed by elucidation of a reasonably contemporaneous grant made of what became the Kenwood and Parliament Hill estates in 1226.[3] Hales, incidentally, places 'Deormod's wick' near the Vale of Health on the line of the ancient, and extant, track which leads from Millfield Lane in Highgate to Well Walk in Hampstead.

The Domesday Survey of 1086 tells us rather less about Hampstead topographically: it chiefly relates what usable or taxable land there was. It details five hides of land in use for arable or grazing, and this could mean anything from 300 to 750 acres, because a hide was an imprecise measurement. Eviden-

# 1. The Eton College Chalcots Estate

# 2. Kilburn Priory Estate

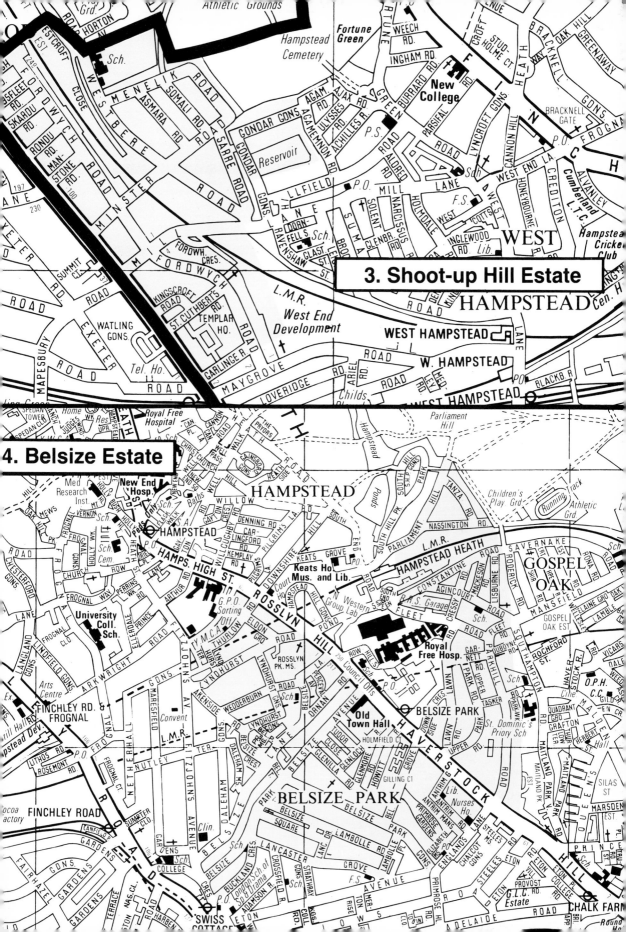

**3. Shoot-up Hill Estate**

**4. Belsize Estate**

*5. Part of the AD 986 Charter granting the Manor of Hampstead to the Abbot of Westminster. The original is now in the British Library.*

tly, therefore, not much of the manor of about 2250 acres was cultivated and, indeed, could not be by a population of only about sixty people.

Fragmentation of the manor occurred by the 12th century. The Hospital of St James for leprous women (on the site of St James's Palace, Westminster), was granted the land subsequently known as the Chalcots or Eton College Estate. This area is described in 1204 as being of one hide, but certainly by 1762 it was about 200 acres.[4] The estate is shown in illustration 1. It was not the only land in Hampstead held by the Hospital. In the 13th century it received two further bequests which made up the 340-acre farm attached to the house later called Old Wyldes at North End.[5] Some of that land was in Hampstead and the rest in Hendon. In 1449 the Hospital and its estates in Hampstead and elsewhere in London were put in the custody of the newly-founded Eton College. Thus, from this date, the connection of the College with Hampstead began, a relationship perpetuated today in the street names and by the College's continued ownership of land.

In the south-west of Hampstead Kilburn Priory, with 224 acres, developed from a 12th-century hermitage, and although a tenancy under the care of the Abbot of Westminster it seems to have acquired separate status by the time it

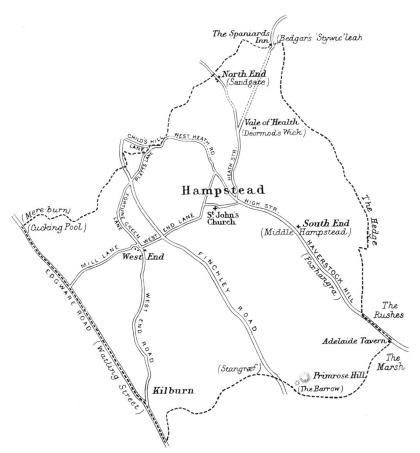

6. *Map by Professor John W. Hales which interprets the topographical content of the AD 986 Charter. Reproduced from the* Transactions *of the London and Middlesex Topographical Society, Old Series, Vol. 6, p. 560.*

was suppressed in 1536. The Priory was not an important one and an inventory of 1535 shows its possessions to be meagre. The estate, shown in illustration 2, was taken by the Crown and granted instead to the Clerkenwell-based Hospital of St John of Jerusalem, but this establishment was itself suppressed in 1540.

The Hospital of St John already had a Hampstead estate of 117 acres, not far up the road to Edgware – what became known as the Shoot-up Hill estate. This land had been given to the Knights Templars in the 13th century. The Templars, a military order whose overt mission was to maintain free access for Christian pilgrims to the Holy Land, became too powerful in the eyes of temporal lords and were disbanded in 1312. Their Hampstead land, and much of their other property in London, went to the Hospital of St John.

Both the Kilburn and the Shoot-up Hill estates were taken by the Crown in 1540 and then disposed of separately. In 1595 Sir Arthur Atye, secretary to the Earl of Leicester, took possession of them both and they remained under one ownership until 1768 when they were sold off separately once more.

The largest fragmentation of the manor occurred at an unknown date. The Belsize area, which stretched across the main road to Hampstead, possibly

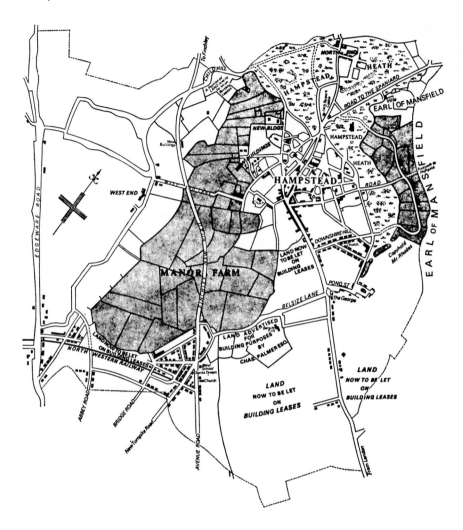

*7. Hampstead in 1853,
showing the two
Maryon Wilson estates
(shaded).*

*8. Remains of Kilburn Priory as it appeared in 1722. Published 1814.*

had sub-manorial status. It is first noted in the will of Sir Roger le Brabazon, who died in 1317, but its existence is possibly implied in the Domesday Survey where one hide of the Hampstead manor is said to be held separately by Ranulf Pevrel under the Abbot of Westminster. Brabazon, a descendant of a Norman who fought at Battle in 1066, was Lord Chief Justice in the reigns of Edward I and Edward II. His will mentions a house and 57 acres[6] at 'Belassis' (French for 'beautifully situated'), but it is not clear if he lived there, nor if the stated acreage was the entire estate or only that land worth mentioning. No record of addition to his estate has since been found and it must be presumed that his holding actually contained the 240-odd acres shown on a 1679 map.

Confusingly, Brabazon left his property to the Abbot of Westminster from whom, presumably, it had been prised in the first place. Despite this unification, at the time of the Dissolution the Hampstead and Belsize manors were treated as two entities and went their own ways in ownership thereafter.

These, then, were the principal detached estates of Hampstead. As to the main manor holding, when development was seriously contemplated in the 19th century, it had been reduced to two areas separated by the Heath and the village centre (see illustration 7). Long custom had put the Heath area into an ill-defined common category: it was still nominally part of the lord of the manor's property and could be encroached upon only with his permission, but the commoners and copyholders who had rights to use the Heath could, and sometimes did, in law, challenge his actions in granting it away or building on it. Encroachment had been going on long before the 19th century, to the benefit of everyone. By the time the Maryon Wilson family had the manor in the 18th century the village, which had previously been around the church and the High Street, extended well into the Heath land.

It may be wondered why the eastern, detached, part of the manor known later as the East Park estate had not also become part of the Heath with a similarly hazy legal status. This is not clear, but its boundary on the west with what was known as the Heath is principally determined by the course of one of the tributaries of the river Fleet, and this may have been the cause of its early separation. Whatever the reason, this small area of land, wedged between the Heath on the west and Kenwood and Parliament Hill to the east, was eligible for development if access and Parliamentary permission could be procured, in much the same way as for the main part of the manor west of the High Street. It was, however, this odd bit of land, remote from the original village, which was the basis of the long battle to save the Heath.[7]

Hampstead's lord of the manor was an absentee. Until the Dissolution, the Abbot of Westminster employed a steward to collect rents, manage the estate and preside at manor courts. Subsequent lay owners preferred to live elsewhere, and from 1707 the family which held the manor until recent times lived in the significant splendour of Charlton House at Greenwich or at the more modest abode of Great Canfield in Essex. Hampstead therefore escaped the familiar twin domination by church and squire. It is not possible to evaluate whether this led to the wealthier residents assuming more responsibilities away from a lord's shadow, although we do know that the resident of Belsize House at the end of the 16th century was a local magistrate.

There was a manor house, however, even if its functions were curtailed through lack of a resident lord. It is mentioned in 1619 as the 'Mannour House, alias Hamsteede Hall' and again, but now split into two residences, in 1762.[8] This division of the house seems to have begun by 1674 when a Benoni Honywood, then aged 76, stated that he dwelt infrequently at the 'manor house of which he was lessee' and that he had let part of it and all of the farm.[9]

The position of the manor house is shown in illustration 9. It was on the north side of Frognal Lane, then called West End Lane. The old parish church faced it, as was right and proper, and a path led from the church porch, past a pond, to the house. The prestige of the manor house remained high enough in 1747 for the architect of the rebuilt church to place the entrance still facing the manor house, despite the fact that the bulk of the congregation came from the other direction.[10] The fact that the lord of the manor still had the living may have had some influence here. The entrance was moved in 1878 with the enlargement and reorientation of St John's.

Most likely, in earlier times, the manor house was used as a vicarage as well as for the steward's headquarters. In the 1550s the vicar was rehoused in a building on the site of No. 28 High Street, and this freed the manor house for the management of Hall Oak Farm, the main manorial property. A plan of that estate in 1762 has three fields called Upper or Lower Purloins. It is tempting to interpret this odd word as a corruption of 'purlieu', which could mean the border of a forest. If this is correct, then the clearing from the forest, hundreds of years earlier, extended to roughly the junction of Finchley and Arkwright Roads, and as far down Fitzjohn's Avenue as Belsize Lane.

[1] Thomas J. Barratt, *The Annals of Hampstead*, Vol. 1, p. 12 (1912).
[2] Professor John W. Hales, *Transactions of the London and Middlesex Archaeological Society*, Old Series, Vol. 6 (1890).
[3] Percy W. Lovell and William McB Marcham, *Survey of London*, Vol. 17, p. 121 (1936).
[4] James Ellis, Terrier to the 1762 map of Hampstead manor.
[5] Philip Venning, *Wyldes; A New History* (1977).
[6] He is also noted in a 1312 Valuation of Hampstead as holding a house and 40 acres. See J. Kennedy, *The Manor and Parish Church of Hampstead and Its Vicars* (1906).
[7] See Chapter 6.
[8] James Ellis, op. cit.
[9] Middlesex Sessions Rolls, June 1674.
[10] Ernest Atkinson, 'Church, Tower and Row' from *The Heathside Book*, ed. Ian Norrie (1962).

# CHAPTER TWO

# The Village Centred

A survey made in 1312[1] shows that there were at least 41 dwellings in Hampstead and 44 named tenants. These included the Roger le Brabazon already mentioned and Robert of 'Kyngeswell', a name perpetuated today in the Heath Street development. There is also a Richard Blakette with a house and 30 acres, and he was probably the owner of what was described in the 17th century as 'Blacketts Well', north west of Branch Hill. Adjoining was a similar-sized property held by Robert Child, whose name survives today in Childs Hill.

These are early sources for place names in Hampstead. Other early names have not been explained satisfactorily. The origin of Shoot-up Hill, mentioned in 1566, remains obscure, as does that of Fortune Green (1646). Similarly Frognal and Haverstock Hill have no convincing explanations.

The 1312 survey also implies the existence of a chapel or church in Hampstead in that 'John de Neuport, clerk' helped to compile the document; in any case, its existence is confirmed in 1333 in another record. A more startling mention is made of an early parish priest, however, in 1384. This has not been remarked on in previous histories of Hampstead (perhaps on grounds of good taste, for it is not difficult to track down). In State papers for that year there is an order to set free John 'the parisshe priest of Hampstede imprisoned at suit of Walter Wodewarde for rape and abduction of Maud his wife at Hampstead, his goods and chattels'.[2] We know no more of this astonishing item than these words, but they suggest, whatever else, that Hampstead by then had a secular priest, rather than a monk, ostensibly looking after its morals.[3]

The parish church was named after St Mary (it is not clear which one) until it was rebuilt in 1747, at which time it became St John's. Its first burial ground to the south of the church is now the oldest in London still left as a graveyard. Like most outer London burial grounds it was overcrowded by the end of the 18th century and in 1812 an extension was formed on the other side of Church Row, using part of a meadow on which Prospect Place had already intruded, and on which St Mary's Roman Catholic church was to be built.

Until the relative affluence of the 16th century there was no reason for Hampstead to have been chosen as a place in which to live in rural delight. The aristocracy had its houses in London or else on its country estates, and a house in a place like Hampstead, near to London, had no advantage. Furthermore, for a large part of the year the weather made Hampstead difficult to travel to and, it may be imagined, cold to endure. It is significant that the only house of aristocratic class that we know of before the 16th century was not in

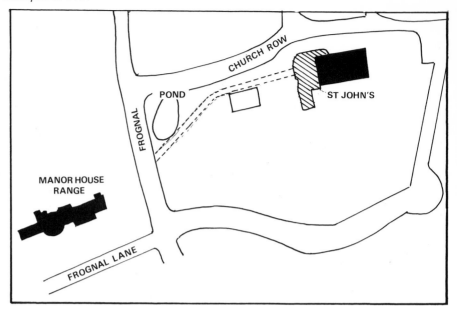

*9. Position of the Manor House, Frognal.*

Hampstead village, but considerably down the hill at Belsize. In 1496 the Abbey of Westminster contracted to produce 400,000 bricks at Belsize. Professor Thompson, who discovered this information, makes the point that it would have been bizarre to have manufactured these in Belsize for use in London as many brickfields lay between, and this fact leads to the conclusion that the bricks were made to build an early form of Belsize House and a wall around it.[4] The house is mentioned in 1550 and rebuilt, reputedly, in 1663. The second, and more famous building, is shown in illustration 11 and its position in illustration 12. A 1679 map also shows a brickfield just north-west of the grounds.

In the 16th century a number of factors led to the expansion of Hampstead and Highgate on the northern ridge. First, the professional institutions such as the Inns of Court, the courts of law and the primitive government departments, developed. In part this was due to the Court becoming less peripatetic and settling for longer periods at Westminster; around the Court its officers, advisers, providers and flatterers remained. Also, the traders and manufacturers, deriving strength from colonial enterprise, were beginning to congregate in specific areas of London, principally to the north. It followed that the wealthier of these various occupations, tied to an unhealthy London for longer periods, would look around for weekend retreats. Highgate and Hampstead provided country rest, scenic beauty and reasonable access except in bad weather.

Hampstead was a village in size. The crossroads of High Street and Heath Street did not exist, although Holly Hill, then called Cloth Hill, did – this was the road to Childs Hill. Between the church and the High Street was a cluster of small buildings and courts which were swept away in the 1880s when Heath Street was extended to meet Fitzjohn's Avenue. This topography may still be seen in the 1814 map, published with Park's book on Hampstead, which is reproduced on p. 6. There were small settlements at Pond Street, North End, West End and South End, but the Hampstead population was almost all contained near the top of the High Street, and did not extend very far up what became Heath Street. Illustration 13 shows the extent of the Heath in 1680, and the name New End, meaning the new part of town, does not appear until 1683.[5] The expansion of the village to the more difficult terrain of this quarter is explained mainly by the cheapness and availability of the Heath land. In any case, expansion here fortuitously coincided with the development of Hampstead Wells in the early 18th century.

In the 17th century, however, there was probably little change in the nature of the village. Parish registers can indicate population trends but it has to be said that those for Hampstead, extant from the very early date of 1560, are confusing. While the number of marriages solemnized each year remained stable at about five for each of the first 137 years, there is a gradual increase in christenings. The burial registers have to be interpreted with care. Many of the burials in the 1630s, and after, are of nurse-children who were farmed out by London parents to be wet-nursed in the healthy air of Hampstead by usually unhealthy foster mothers – a similar cottage industry prevailed in Highgate.[6] In 1665, the year of the Great Plague in London, the burials shot up from the usual average of 32 to over 140. It is generally assumed that a large number of people from London settled in such places as Hampstead following the catastrophic events of 1665–6 and awaited the rebuilding of London, but the odd thing is that the Hampstead registers, except in the Plague year, do not show a significant number of 'strangers' until after 1669.

Perhaps the number of public houses is the best indication of the vitality of a village, rather than the activities surrounding church or manor house.

*10. View of the Old Church at Hampstead. Publ. 1785.*

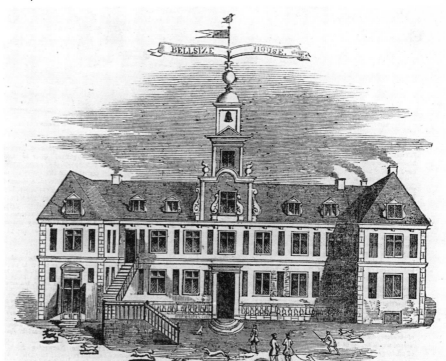

11. *Belsize House. An
18th-century view
reproduced in the*
Illustrated London
News, *9 Sept. 1854.*

12. *Position of Belsize
House. Drawn from
information kindly
supplied by Roy Allen.*

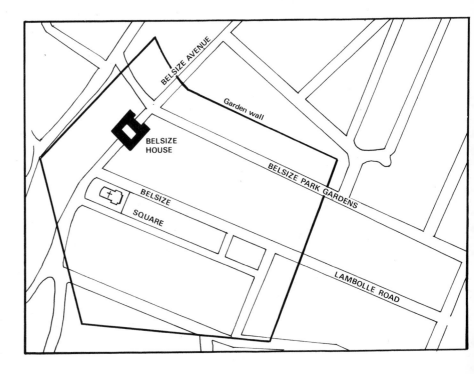

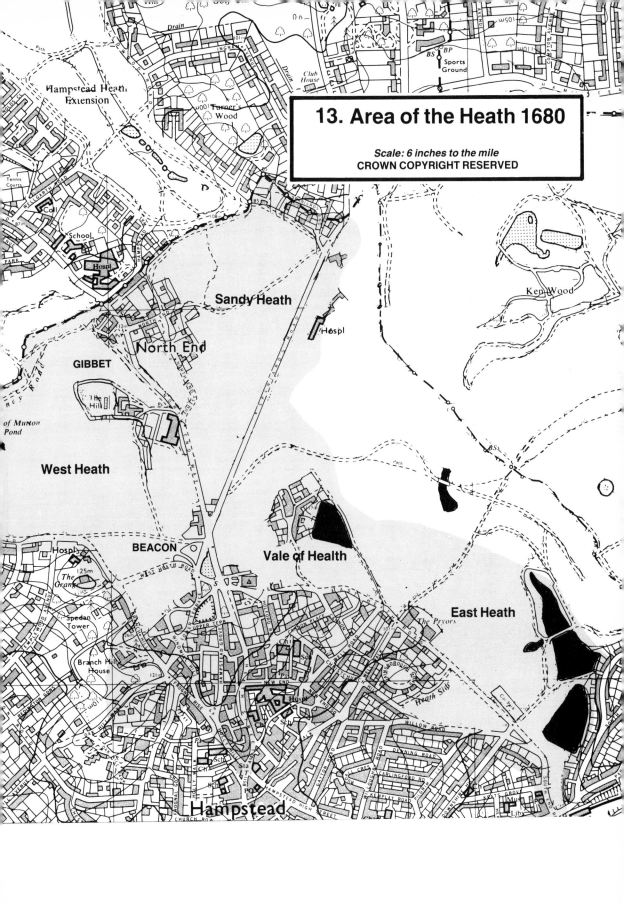

## 13. Area of the Heath 1680

Scale: 6 inches to the mile
CROWN COPYRIGHT RESERVED

According to a Middlesex Session record of 1633, Hampstead had six ale-houses, of which three were to be suppressed. These did not include inns which offered lodging, nor taverns which sold wine, and so this first record is not much of a guide to 17th-century drinking habits. The first public houses in Hampstead we know about were, in fact, disreputable alehouses. One Thomas Roberts was arraigned several times between 1609 and 1615 for keeping a disorderly house – meaning, it seems, drunken rather than immoral.[7] In 1641 two houses were suppressed because of Sunday drinking on the premises, and in 1653 another was banned due to continual disorders and a death resulting from a fight there. None of these properties is named.

Victuallers had an easier time after the Restoration, so much so that in 1667 the minister and churchwardens applied to the magistrates to suppress nine alehouses in Hampstead, leaving, one hopes, others still open. Numbers rose again sharply during the Hampstead Wells period and by 1721 there were 26 licensed premises.

To hazard which inns, taverns or alehouses existed in the village in the 17th century, we should assume that they were on the High Street or in the alleyways off it, and outside the area of the Heath as shown in the map of *c*.1680.[8] Therefore, what became Heath Street is excluded. Useful licensing records begin in 1721, by which time there were seven drinking places within this village area. Three of them have now gone altogether: the White Hart lay back from the High Street roughly on the line of Gayton Road and it was described as ruinous when it was demolished *c*.1820; the Three Tuns, closed in 1778, stood at No. 14 High Street next to the Hampstead Brewery; the Kings Arms was on the site of No. 31 High Street and probably extended over the tiny passageway still to be observed next door. This inn, which ceased trading in 1780 when the owner of No. 32 extended his premises into it, must surely be a candidate for the earliest inn in Hampstead village – it had a much-coveted name and a capacious prime position (its yard later provided part of the room required for a horse bus terminus and the Blue Star Garage). The Kings Head, later renamed the King William IV, on the route from manor house and church to vicarage and High Street, must also contend for longevity for similar reasons. The Three Horseshoes, contained in the cluster of courtyards west of the High Street, was relocated when the centre of Hampstead was rebuilt in the 1880s. The first inn name we find recorded is that of the King of Bohemia, mentioned in 1680.[9] The Flask, provided that its name did not supplant another, would have been established during the Wells period. If these were the earliest establishments in the village then the Nags Head in Heath Street was not far behind – it is noted in 1698.[10]

Elsewhere in the parish there were several other inns which might have been 17th-century. On the road up to Hampstead village was the Load of Hay, still there near the foot of Haverstock Hill. It had an important position at the bottom of a long hill and its name, together with its previous one of Cart and Horses, suggests a staging post before the long haul. Halfway up was, and is, the George, mentioned in 1715 and previously called the Great Tree.[11] In the hamlet of West End the earliest inn was the Black Lion, there by 1721 at least, as too was the Bull and Bush at North End. At the bottom of Pond Street, the White Horse was also trading in 1721, and on the Spaniards Road, on the

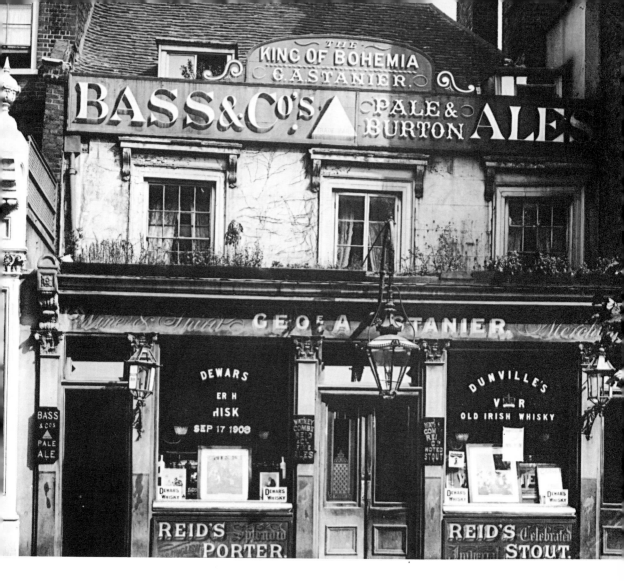

14. The King of Bohemia, Hampstead High Street. Photograph, Sept. 1903.

site of The Elms, was a place called Mother Huff's, principally a tea-garden but also licensed for the sale of alcohol. When its owner left in 1728 she claimed that she had established it fifty years previously and it is, indeed, noted on a 1680 map of the Heath. In Kilburn the Red Lion, Black Lion and Bell were almost certainly 17th-century, and even earlier is claimed for the Red Lion.

Until shops usurped them in the 18th century, it was the inns which sold general provisions. Not many local traders appear in early records and, significantly, those that do provided services that inns normally wouldn't. In the 1613–16 period there were a tailor, sawyer, miller and blacksmith, and in the decade before tile-makers were also mentioned. There were mills at Mount Vernon and Hampstead Grove[12] but there was also a mill house west of the High Street on the site of the present apex with lower Heath Street. By 1776, when it is mentioned in the court rolls, it had become a brewhouse run jointly by Robert Vincent with his Hampstead Brewery lower down the High Street.[13] There was another windmill at the junction of Mill Lane and Edgware Road.

23

*15. Windmill at the junction of Mill Lane and Edgware Road. Burnt down 1861.*

Undoubtedly the main occupation of the Hampstead working-class was agriculture, with others making bricks or tiles. In 1653 local residents asked the Parliamentary Commissioners, who were intent on taxing them, 'to remember [the] poverty of the place. Many are poore labouring men on wages at the Tyle-kilns and other places, and their wives washing clothes for London. Divers houses are occupied by citizens of London, who pay there.'[14] This illuminating comment bears witness not just to the poverty and the early occupation of laundering in Hampstead but to a village which had become a place for country houses.

But where were these country houses, presumably grander than the locals could afford, in the 17th century? In 1664 twelve houses with ten hearths and over were taxed, the largest having 24. It has not been possible, so far, to identify any of them positively, and so it is interesting to look at Highgate, where we do know many of the houses, to get some idea of the size of houses in the hearth tax return. Lauderdale House on Highgate Hill, smaller then than it is today, was taxed on 23 hearths, and so the largest Hampstead house, if we are to believe the Hampstead return, was hardly bigger than this.

This seems to conflict with the pictorial evidence. For example, Belsize House was a very large property and it was reputedly rebuilt in 1663 by a Colonel Daniel O'Neill, made rich by rewards of lands and monopolies for backing the right horse in the Civil War. In the Hearth Tax return he is taxed for only seven hearths and in that year he died. Perhaps the house was then in

the early stages of construction. Vane House, a much larger house than Lauderdale's, was also built by 1664. Sir Harry Vane had not been quite sure which horse to back during that tumultuous period – he was a republican at odds with both Cromwell and Charles I and was to pay for his indecisiveness when Charles II came to the throne. In June 1660 a company of soldiers marched up the road to Hampstead and took him away to the Tower of London; he was then imprisoned for two years in the Scilly Isles before he faced a London trial as biased as most in that period. The execution was in June 1662.

*16. Sir Henry Vane's house at Hampstead. Engraving by W. Davison, publ. 1813.*

Across the High Street from him was the Chicken House. We do not know the derivation of the odd name, or why James I, together with Buckingham, stayed there in 1619, or why a stained-glass window commemorated that visit, or who owned the house at the time. The property, depicted in illustrations 17 and 63, gradually went down in the social scale, became a public house briefly in 1759 and was finally demolished *c*.1888. Nearby was what became Carlile House. In 1692 Isaac Honywood was licensed to hold meetings of dissenters at this house.

Other large houses of the time included Holly Hill House on the site of the garden of the junior University College School; its door and staircase were incorporated into the present school building. Off Frognal, on the site of the tennis court belonging to the Medical Research Council, was a building which served as the first Hampstead workhouse. It housed the poor by 1729 but in the manor court rolls for 1700 there is a mention of a 'Parish House' which could have been the same place.

Scant record remains of more ordinary dwellings, and even less of their occupiers. The names of the poor usually come to light if substantial charities left records of their largesse. However, there were no such bodies in the 17th century. The parish was responsible for those in dire need, and it does not seem to have been particularly generous. A woman went to the magistrates in 1674 to plead that with her husband in prison she could not afford to support her three children and her mother-in-law, but the churchwardens of Hampstead had refused her aid. In this case the magistrates ordered them to be merciful. Two years later, a lame, deaf and dumb child, abandoned by his mother, was sent back to Dorset where he was born: in this the churchwardens were adhering strictly to the Settlement laws.

Not only were the poor laws brutish – so was the justice. Thieves were usually hanged. In 1614 two women stole clothes from a house at West End and one was hanged. But William Deane, who broke into Belsize House in 1608 and stole silver-plate from, of all people, the local magistrate and high official at Court, Sir William Waad, managed to escape death by reading 'as a Clerk'; he was branded instead. Not so literate or fortunate was William Boden, who stole goods to the high value of £13 from John Raynes, gentleman of Hampstead, in 1609; he was executed. As late as 1750 a man called Nightingale Head was whipped from the Red Lion on Rosslyn Hill to the Upper Flask near Whitestone Pond for an offence and then transported to America. These were not abnormal punishments for the time. The fate of malefactors was symbolized by the gibbet in North End Way on which the corpses of executed criminals were displayed for years.

*17. The Chicken House, Hampstead High Street. 18th-century view.*

The poor of Hampstead had no schooling. They were unlucky in that a sometime resident, Sir Roger Cholmeley, decided to spend his declining years in Highgate instead, and it was there he founded his Free School in 1565. The earliest Hampstead school we know of was actually in a tree. One of the 17th-century attractions of Hampstead was the Hollow Elm, somewhere on the summit of the Heath, which contained a staircase of forty-two steps leading to a turret which could seat six and have fourteen standing. Barratt records that a school for twelve young gentlemen was held here in the middle of the 17th century.[15] Apart from that, the first land-based school in Hampstead of which we have record was that run by Lancelott Johnson in 1684; he was allowed to plant trees between his school and the Heath 'for the protection and comfort of the scholars there and with a certain hedge to protect the same from cattle.'[16] This was probably on a site at New End.

The lack of education and the general credulity of the people of this period encouraged a belief in witchcraft – probably every village in England could cite its own examples. In Hampstead's case a woman was arraigned in 1605 for practising witchcraft on the body of another woman who 'languished and wasted in her body' and also on a young boy and on some heifers and hogs. In 1614, a married couple called Hunt faced the same sort of accusation; they appeared before Sir William Waad, who dismissed the charge – to the dismay of the woman who had brought it. She accused Waad of having 'slubbered up the matter of witchcrafte', use of which verb resulted in her having to apologise to the magistrate and to produce a written affidavit that she had. The

*18. 'The Hollow Elme of Hampsted' (after Wenceslaus Hollar, 1653).*

Hunts were charged again, however, and appeared at the Old Bailey. Once more they were acquitted, but in 1615 Joan Hunt, again charged, was found guilty and sentenced to death.

[1] J. Kennedy, *The Manor and Parish Church of Hampstead and Its Vicars* p. 112 (1906).
[2] Close Rolls, 24 June 1384.
[3] J. Kennedy, op. cit., suggests that secular priests began in 1551.
[4] Professor F. M. L. Thompson, *Hampstead: Building a Borough 1650–1964*, p. 8 (1974).
[5] Hampstead parish burial register, 1683.
[6] John Richardson, *Highgate: Its History Since the Fifteenth Century* p. 24 (1983).
[7] Middlesex Sessions Records, 1609 and 1615.
[8] See illustration 13.
[9] Thomas J. Barratt, op. cit., Vol. 1, p. 195.
[10] Hampstead Manor Court Rolls, 6 June 1698.
[11] Ibid, 30 May 1715.
[12] Alan Farmer, *Hampstead Heath* p. 16 (1984)
[13] Hampstead Manor Court Rolls, 12 September 1776.
[14] Parliamentary Assessment of landholders in Hampstead, 12 December 1653. Bodleian Library MS, Rawlinson D715 f81, reprinted in Barratt, op. cit., Vol. 3, p. 363.
[15] Thomas J. Barratt, op. cit., Vol. 1, pp. 168–71.
[16] Hampstead Manor Court Rolls, 12 May 1684.

# CHAPTER THREE

# Expansion at the Ends

When the New River Company brought its clean water from Hertfordshire to London in 1613 the demand was not encouraging. In the same century the City of London only half-heartedly exercised its concession to use the ponds and springs of Highgate and Hampstead to bring fresh water to the City. However, it must be conceded that it was not all that drinkable. People of all ages drank small-ale instead, and they bathed infrequently. It was therefore the equivalent of a modern-day health fad which made medicinal waters popular. The chalybeate wells of Tunbridge in Kent attracted aristocratic palates and gradually people were persuaded that various maladies might be cured by the 'waters'.

The Hampstead wells were part of the first generation of London spas. Chronologically, Streatham, established in 1660, was the first of any note, but a shrewd surveyor of local highways, Sadler, rediscovered a medicinal spring in Islington in the early 1680s and added another ingredient – entertainment. His 'musick-house' made the awful taste of his water acceptable, and this forerunner of Sadler's Wells Theatre set the pattern for the London spas.

Alas for the proprietors, some successful wells became disreputable also. They were near enough to London for the socially unacceptable to visit, and the owners faced the dilemma of making money quickly while the fad was at its height or maintaining an upright social tone into an unpredictable future.

In December 1698 the lord of the manor of Hampstead, the 13-year-old Earl of Gainsborough, granted through his mother, six acres of land including 'the wells lately made there for medicinal waters' to the poor of Hampstead. In effect, trustees were appointed to make what they could out of the place but without the funds to do so properly. The estate, shown in illustration 19, slopes steeply from Well Road; it was partly swamp at the time, which appears to have been typical of the area as we read of a parcel of waste nearby at New End described as a 'boggy piece of ground' in 1716. It was not a promising gift, although the wells already had a reputation which may have stretched back to the middle of the previous century. Michael Sparkes, a minor poet, writing c.1650 about the Hollow Elm, tantalisingly mentions a well in the vicinity, and coin tokens of 1669–70 portray one. The new spa was, however, sufficiently established by 1697 for Celia Fiennes to comment on its plumbing.[1]

The trustees of the estate claimed the waters to be equal to those of Tunbridge and advertised them in 1700 as being available at 3d per flask at the Eagle and Child apothecary in Fleet Street, to which they were transported each day. Evidently this was not profitable enough, and in the same year the

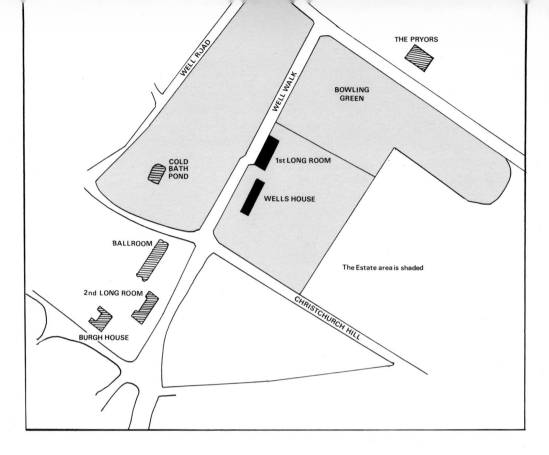

THE PRYORS

WELL ROAD

WELL WALK

BOWLING
GREEN

COLD
BATH
POND

1st LONG ROOM

WELLS HOUSE

BALLROOM

The Estate area is shaded

2nd LONG ROOM

CHRISTCHURCH HILL

BURGH HOUSE

*19. The Wells estate
area in 1762.*

trustees put the estate up for speculation. One John Duffield took up the
concession with the financial backing of a business colleague. The right to sell
the water in flasks was kept by the trustees and this was sold at the Flask
Tavern.

The actual spring was near what is now Well Road; by this was the Cold
Bath Pond. The water was fed down to Duffield's Great or Long Room,
erected on the more level ground of Well Walk; in this building were a section
for drinking the waters and another for amusements such as dancing, music
and gambling. On the walls were life-size paintings of the muses.[2] An
ice-house (still extant, in the present Gainsborough Gardens) was probably
built at the same time.

The clientèle must have been affluent some of the time – for a concert
advertised in 1701 the entrance fee was five shillings, a large sum in those
days. The spa was profitable enough, anyway, to erect a 'Cold Bath', presumably a bathing-house near the Cold Bath Pond, in 1705, and to provide a
bowling green and build a tavern at first called the Green Man (this has been
superseded by the Wells Tavern).

None of this appears to have benefited the poor, as Duffield did not pay his
rent and the trustees neglected their responsibility to collect it. Typical of their
ill-management was the use of the spring water by John Vincent of the
Hampstead Brewery. He laid pipes from the spring to his premises in the
High Street and elsewhere, but it was some years before any payments were
extracted from him. The pipes were found when construction of Gayton Road
was in progress, but it may be wondered what the water was used for. It had,
by all accounts, a strong taste and it would have been unsuitable for beer.

The Wells had their heyday and then lost favour as the better-off withdrew in the face of the disreputable company to patronise attractions elsewhere. Duffield made some money out of it: he is reported, in 1706, to have built a brick house in Hampstead, which has been wrongly identified as Foley House in East Heath Road.[3]

It is not clear when his Long Room closed, but by 1725 it had been converted into a chapel by a Joseph Rous.[4] In the second period of the Wells new assembly rooms were built on the other side of Well Walk next to Burgh House and outside the area of the Wells estate, but these were not in use until *c.*1734. It is contended that the waters, if not the entertainment, were still enjoyed during the time between the closing and opening of these two buildings. 'The fountain, basin, and fittings [were] removed from the great or long room, and apparently fitted up in a building called the Wells House . . .'[5] The origins and functions of this building remain obscure. It is possible that it is referred to in a Middlesex Sessions record of 1722: 'At Hampstead Wells they have . . . built a large room for using and carrying on divers kinds of unlawful games . . . which manifestly tend to the encouragement of vice and immorality, and to the debauching and ruining of servants, apprentices and others . . . They keep great numbers of persons who pretend to be soldiers in order to prevent the civil magistrates from apprehending and punishing . . .'

Clearly, things had got out of hand by then and residents, other than the tradespeople, were probably glad to see the spa close down. They had already complained in 1709 about a playhouse in the vicinity. The vicar and churchwardens, with others who were morally outraged, had been to the magistrates, who threatened the performers with the statute which described 'common players of interludes to be rogues, vagabonds and sturdy beggars' and which prescribed pain and punishment for their offence. But the following year the players were back and the magistrates decided to arrest them.[6]

The court rolls do not mention the new assembly rooms until 1753, but we have to thank a letter written by Alexander Pope in 1734, about a visit to his friend Dr Arbuthnot, for an earlier indication of their existence: 'I spent a whole day with him at Hampstead. He was in the Long Room half the morning and has parties at cards every night.'[7] By then the old Long Room was a chapel and Dr Arbuthnot must have been in a new building. As shown in illustration 19, it fronted the western side of Well Walk and to its side and rear was a ballroom. These buildings were visited not only by Pope but by Samuel Johnson, Mrs Thrale and Fanny Burney.

About 1803 the second Long Room became a private residence and Hampstead's spa days were over. The owner in the 1870s encased it in red brick and dressed it up as a Queen Anne mansion, although the interior was sensitively restored.

Despite the fame of both Long Rooms there is little visual record of them. A 19th-century artist recorded the first building a few years before its demolition in 1882 (see title pages), and that is virtually all we have of it. The second Long Room and its ballroom are shown, rather indistinctly, in Chatelaine's 1745 view from Willow Road, with Burgh House recognisable to the left (illustration 20). There is also a drawing of the second Long Room after it had its red-brick coat, and illustration 22 is a 1944 photograph of the old ballroom

20. 'A Prospect of the Long Room at Hampstead from the Heath'. By Chatelain, 1745. Burgh House is visible in the centre of the picture, and to the right is the second Long Room and the ballroom.

21. The second Long Room in Well Walk, 1912, now called Weatherall House. From a drawing by A. R. Quinton, reproduced from Barratt's Annals of Hampstead (1912).

*22. Photograph of Nos. 7–9 Well Walk, the old ballroom in 1944.*

when it had been converted into separate houses.

Given the dearth of illustrations some writers have been relieved to find a festive occasion at the second Long Room supposedly depicted on an 18th-century fan (illustration 23). The occasion was in September 1754, when Thomas Osborne, a London bookseller, held a breakfast party at a house he rented in Hampstead, with a duck-shoot on the Heath afterwards and festivities at the Long Room. It has to be said that none of the buildings shown on the fan looks remotely like any illustration we have of the second Long Room or its adjoining buildings, and it has been suggested that the artist was exercising considerable licence. This is unfair to the artist, because the illustrations are not of the Long Room at all – they are of Norway House, off the High Street, on what became, in modern times, the Blue Star site.

The clue to this solution is given in the terrier of the 1762 map of Hampstead in which Thomas Osborne is listed for 'one other house backwards [meaning back from] the [High] Street with coachhouse, stable, outhouses and necessarys, a yard and large garden, a summer house therein . . .' The map and its terrier make clear that this is what became Norway House, a range of buildings at right-angles to the High Street, with views over the Heath and gardens down to Willow Road. Illustration 24 is a drawing of part of Norway House as depicted in Barratt and can be compared with one of the houses that appears on the fan.

The second Long Room and the houses converted from the old ballroom were damaged in the last war and were demolished, despite protests, in the utopian year of 1948; the present local authority block, Wells House, was erected on their sites.

*23. The two sides of the fan made to commemorate Mr Osborne's Hampstead party in 1754.*

During the first Wells period Hampstead offered another attraction to the curious of London – Belsize House. About 1700, Charles Povey, a retired coal-merchant and inveterate inventor, was sub-tenant. He opened up the house and gardens to the public and, in addition, provided a private Sion chapel in which a parson could quickly wed a couple armed with the right documents and, it is implied, without them if necessary. Deer-hunting was also a speciality.

Belsize House had mainly aristocratic tenants in the 16th and 17th centuries, the last one being Lord Wotton, who inherited in 1666 and died in 1682. He is said to have improved both the property and the large gardens, but Pepys, who saw the gardens in 1668, was rather sniffy about them.

*24. Norway House, off Hampstead High Street, 1911. From a drawing by A. R. Quinton, reproduced in Barratt's* Annals of Hampstead *(1912).*

Thereafter came sub-tenants of no particular note until Povey, and once he had tired of his venture there came in 1720 a sub-sub-tenant, a Welshman called Howell who, with some style and flair, completely vulgarised the place.

His new entertainments at Belsize House began well enough and even enticed the Prince of Wales to visit in 1721; for a time it outshone the better-known Vauxhall and Ranelagh Gardens. Howell proclaimed in 1723: 'Bellsize House is open every day; the public days are Mondays, Thursdays and Saturdays, with a good Concert of Musick in the Long Gallery during the whole season. The Proprietor is now provided with a Pack of good staunch Hounds, and a Huntsman, ready to show the Diversion of Hunting whenever the Company pleases; the Walks in the Garden and Parks are made very pleasant, where Gentlemen and Ladies have frequent Egress and Regress to Walk without any Expence. Any company that stays late,' he added, 'there are Servants with Fire-Arms to see them safe to London.'[8]

The armed guard was a familiar item in London – many of the outlying districts organised convoys of wary travellers at certain times of the day. Howell did not mention the race-course, which probably came later, or the sexual attractions which were probably there from the start. A satirist of 1722 makes it plain:

> The scandalous lewd house that's called Belsize,
> Where sharpers lurk, yet Vice in publick lies,
> Is publicly become a Rendezvous,
> Of Strumpets, common as in common Stews . . .[9]

Not to be outdone, a speculator in Kilburn in 1714 decided to exploit the mildly chalybeate spring there – its site is marked at No. 42 Kilburn High Road. The landlord of the Bell sold flasks of the water and a tea-house was set up nearby. It was a more sedate affair than Hampstead Wells – at least, it did not attract the attentions of the magistrates. In 1733 an advertisement claimed that 'The Whole is now opened for the reception of the public, the great room being particularly adapted to the use and amusement of the politest companies, fit for music, dancing or entertainments.'

Kilburn Wells did not last very long. Nor did a pleasure-garden called New Georgia behind the Spaniards. This was constructed 'as a series of practical jokes' devised by one Robert Caston who sourly, and without humour, inscribed on one of the buildings (a cottage which contained a pillory from which a gentleman could only be released by a lady's kiss), the words: 'I, Robert Caston, begun this place in a wild wood . . . stubbed up the wood, digged all the ponds, cut all the walks, made all the gardens, built all the rooms with my own hands. Nobody drove a nail here, or laid a brick, or a tile, but myself; and . . . thank God for giving me strength at sixty-four years ago, when I began it . . .' Mr Caston's self-congratulated endeavours were all in vain: begun in 1737, on Rocque's map of 1745, it was gone by the time of the 1762 map.

The parish Vestry must have been very stretched at this period, especially in the matter of law and order, for the number of visitors and taverns must have overwhelmed the primitive system of spare-time constables and the aged watchmen and beadles. The Vestry was an open one, that is, any male resident who paid poor rates could attend and vote. This system lasted right

*25. Kilburn Wells by the Bell Inn. Published in the* Universal Magazine, *Oct. 1797.*

up to 1855, by which time Hampstead was a town. The Vestry had few statutory funds – indeed few statutory duties. Main roads, education, public health and building permissions were outside its province, although it could certainly bring pressure to bear when aroused. It was happy to aid the magistrates in restricting alehouse hours; it used the magistrates to prevent cabs waiting for hire at the top of the High Street in 1783; it persuaded the New River Company to resite its proposed reservoir at Whitestone Pond in 1854 because it would 'disfigure the Heath'. Even to perform duties which were traditionally the Vestry's required special Acts of Parliament. About 1740 a 'Rogues and Felons Society' was established in Hampstead to protect life and property, but in 1775 it was decided to light the village and provide proper watchmen. An Act of Parliament was introduced and passed, but the Vestry did not carry out this duty – a trust was formed which was empowered to collect a separate rate, and to administer the lighting and watching. Similarly, to rebuild the church or workhouse required special legislation.

This incapacity to govern was not unusual – worse problems existed at nearby St Pancras, but there, at least, residents had voted themselves a Select Vestry system which had more powers. Hampstead decided against such a transition in 1826 and the Vestry was therefore, in 1855 when it was forcibly reformed, an irrelevant body when it came to the administration of a built-up area.

The principal officers of the open Vestry were unpaid – the constables, the overseers of the poor and the surveyors of the highways were obliged to serve terms of office regardless of their suitability. Some applied to the magistrates to be excused and from 1784 the Vestry allowed this on payment of a 10-guinea fine, which was all right for the affluent but a deterrent at a time when a normal wage was £15 per annum. Paid officers included a vestry clerk, the master and matron of the workhouse and the beadle; in addition, sums were paid to collectors of the rates, the sexton, an apothecary to the poor and an old man who taught the workhouse children to read for 10/- per month.[10]

The Vestry had a watch-house which served as a temporary gaol. This was erected in 1707 at the bottom end of Heath Street opposite the present-day Underground station. It projected into the road and in 1748 it was described as an 'inconvenient obstruction' and in a very ruinous state. It was decided to erect a new one elsewhere.[11] The next one was at the bottom of Flask Walk on a small stretch of public wasteland. A small two-cell building with stocks was built; this was made redundant with the establishment of the Metropolitan Police in 1830 and taken down in 1839.[12] There was also a lock-up in the grounds of Cannon Hall, which is still there and marked with a plaque in Cannon Lane.

The overseers of the poor had the most onerous tasks. They were responsible, overall, for the collection of the poor rate so that the workhouse, poor-houses and pensions might be maintained. The workhouse in Frognal had twenty inmates in 1731, nearly half of them children. In 1736 the cost of it was £136 per annum, but offset against that was the value of the garden produce and the labour of the inmates.[13] The workhouse was contained in a Tudor building in Frognal depicted in illustration 64 and it was at one of the lease-renewal times, 1757, that the Vestry decided it would be cheaper to board out the poor elsewhere with a pension, instead of incarcerating them in

*26. The watch-house and stocks at the bottom of Flask Walk, 1831. From a drawing by A. R. Quinton reproduced from Barratt's* Annals of Hampstead *(1912).*

one building. The view was mistaken and the following year the Vestry, alarmed by the increase in cost, was obliged to renew its lease of the crumbling building at a higher rent. By 1779 the house was ruinous and in the possession of a Mr Flitcroft, heir to the architect Henry Flitcroft, who lived nearby. At last, in 1799, the Vestry decided to provide new accommodation. One choice was to buy the Tudor building and build afresh on the site, but the Vestry found that the owner, still Flitcroft, was by then a certified lunatic and his trustees all dead, so there was no one with whom the Vestry could negotiate. Instead, the Vestry bought a house in New End formerly occupied by James Pilgrim, who gave his name to Pilgrim's Lane; it was then owned by a Mrs Leggatt, and cost £1200. Around this the workhouse was enlarged; its site today is covered by the New End Hospital.

There were also parish poor-houses in Pond Street and in the Vale of Health. Those in the Vale were erected a year after the swamp was drained in 1777, and the occupants were transferred from more cramped conditions in houses behind Jack Straw's Castle.

Charities financed some poor relief. The Campden charity, founded by Lady Campden in 1642, had land at Childs Hill in Hendon which provided income. The Wells charity, already mentioned, had six acres which gradually became valuable; these charities merged in 1874 and are still administered by trustees. This amalgamation was joined in 1971 by the John Stock bequest; Stock, who lived at The Mount, left money for the education and clothing of poor children in 1781. Thomas Rumsey made a bequest in 1798 which provided coal at Christmas-time for the poor.

It was an indication of the growing population and its aspirations that the Vestry decided to rebuild the parish church. The medieval building could seat only 366 people – not enough for the residents, let alone the visitors. It was also known to be structurally unsound. One imagines, too, that the Vestry was conscious of the social inadequacy of the old building at a time when the parish was attracting illustrious visitors and when much church-building was taking place in London. If Shoreditch and Bethnal Green could have presti-

n del                                                                    J. Roberts scu

gious new buildings, why not Hampstead with its richer population? Henry Flitcroft, local resident and architect of St Giles-in-the-Fields and Woburn Abbey, was the obvious choice for designer of a new building, and he appeared before a meeting of the Vestry in 1744. The minutes note: 'Mr Flitcroft appear'd according to Request and offer'd to give in a Plan and Estimate of the Church Gratis if he had no competitor, but in Case of a competitor he would not have anything to do with it.'[14]

Bravely, the Vestry decided to go ahead with a competition. It chose another local resident, John Saunderson, who lived at Parkgate, a house near the Spaniards. His tower was much admired, and even inspired a preservation committee in the 1870s, but it was not long before it was found to be unsafe. The new parish church was dedicated to St John – again, as with its previous dedication to St Mary, it is not clear which one.

Apart from two chapels it was the only church in Hampstead at the time. The earliest chapel for dissenters arose from a licence granted in 1692 to Isaac Honywood, Esquire, who lived in what was later called Carlile House, to hold meetings at his home.[15] This was probably a Presbyterian congregation. We do not know at what date it moved from his house to a chapel building in his garden, but a stone found on the site of the old chapel was inscribed with the date 1736 – four years before Honywood died. The other chapel in Hampstead was in the first Long Room in Well Walk, converted, as previously mentioned, in 1725. It was managed by a Church of England preacher and it was to here that the parish church congregation decamped while its own church was being rebuilt in 1745–7.

*27. The south-east view of Hampstead church. Engraving by Chatelain, 1750.*

28. *Upper Heath
(formerly the Upper
Flask), Heath Street.
From a water colour by
A. R. Quinton, 1910.*

29. *Rosslyn Hill
Chapel, 1911. From a
drawing by A. R.
Quinton, reproduced
from Barratt's* Annals
of Hampstead
*(1912).*

*30. Sir Richard Steele's cottage, Haverstock Hill, publ. by J. Tallis.*

The location of the Well Walk chapel underlines the expansion of Hampstead at New End. But despite the Wells, the Heath, the pleasure-gardens and the views across the spires and roofs of London, it can not be said that the rich *and* notable marked out plots on this particular height. There was an increase in population, yes, and some of it was wealthy, but it was not particularly distinguished.

As if in readiness for a large influx, the Upper Flask public house was established in the early years of the century at the top of Heath Street, just south of the junction with what became East Heath Road. It had over an acre of ground newly taken from the Heath, roughly equivalent to the grounds of today's training centre for medical staff. It was here that the well-known Kit-Cat Club held summer meetings in the first decade of the 18th century. Ostensibly a London literary and artistic social club, it also espoused the Protestant and Hanoverian cause, and with the succession of George I, the Club petered out. Its 48 illustrious members included Steele, Addison, Vanbrugh and Marlborough, but their only connection with Hampstead, apart from Steele's brief sojourn at a cottage on Haverstock Hill opposite the Load of Hay in 1712, was this occasional meeting-place in the summer.

Given its site, it is surprising that the Upper Flask did not survive as a tavern – it lasted until *c.*1751, when it became a private house called Upper Heath, three years after it had been immortalised in Samuel Richardson's *Clarissa*. Perhaps the trade from the visitors to the Wells had slackened, or the competition from the many alehouses was too much – Jack Straw's Castle, depicted in illustration 68, developed from three cottages by 1713 and was already well-known. More likely, by that time, the appetite for large, scenically privileged, houses outstripped the economic rewards of running a public house.

Upper Heath became the home of George Steevens, literary scholar, from 1769 until his death in 1800. It is said that he walked to London many mornings to arrive by seven, to see his publisher Tonson, which is very early to see a publisher, or to see literary acquaintances such as Dr Johnson, with whom he collaborated in producing a famous annotated edition of Shakespeare. Coincidentally, Tonson was a descendant of the secretary of the Kit-Cat Club. In literary circles Steevens was largely unpopular because of his spitefulness; Lord Mansfield once remarked that one could only believe half of what he said, and Dr Johnson added that no one could tell which half deserved the credence. In his later years Steevens became a recluse, shunning all local contact.

By the time Steevens moved in, villa building in Hampstead was in full swing and a number of distinguished houses on this ridge were neighbours. Just down the track in East Heath Road was a house called Heathfield, on the site of the present Ladywell Court. In the 1830s it was the home of Charles Holford, one of the noted Hampstead worthies, and through whose grounds Holford Road is formed. In Cannon Place was the splendid Cannon Hall, still extant, which dates from c.1720 and which was an earlier home of the Holford family. The cannon were supplied by Sir James Cosmo Melville, Secretary to the East India Company, a 19th-century resident. South of the Steevens property was Vine House, the present-day No. 6 Hampstead Square. The Square itself is hardly evident now because Christ Church and Nos. 10–12 Hampstead Square occupy most of its area.

Another early settler was Joshua Squire, a factor at the trading house in

*31. Cottages in East Heath Road and Squire's Mount, c.1840. From a lithograph by G. Childs.*

*32. The Pryors, East Heath Road. Drawing by E. Stamp, Feb. 1902.*

*33. Fenton House, 1911. From a drawing by A. R. Quinton, reproduced from Barratt's* Annals of Hampstead

London called Blackwell Hall. He built his house at what became Squire's Mount in 1714. Further down was half an acre taken from the Heath, on which a house later called the Pryors was built; this is now covered by two blocks of flats of the same name. Across the road from Steevens a number of handsome houses went up during the first half of the 18th century, such as Old and New Grove Houses, now Nos. 26 and 28 Hampstead Grove. In the Grove also is the earliest building still standing in Hampstead – Fenton House, built in 1693 and called, by 1703, Ostend House. A possible reason for that name is that it was at the east end of Hampstead (Hampstead is full of 'ends') and it was an unusual way of welcoming William of Orange. Philip Fenton, a merchant, bought it in 1793. Around the corner, in Admiral's Walk, Admiral's House and Grove Lodge were both built *c.* 1700. The house, and the road it is in, were named in the 20th century in the mistaken belief that its nautical features indicated the residence of Admiral Barton, but the embellishments were, in fact, added by a Captain Fountain North after 1774.[16]

Above Heath Street are Nos. 5 and 6 The Mount, possibly built in 1694. An entry in the court rolls of that year records that George Hampfield Esquire was granted leave to a parcel of waste 'now fenced in a circular form called the Mount'. George Romney bought the house in 1796 for £2500 before he embarked on the studios to the rear. Further out, but still high up, was Bleak Hall, later called Branch Hill Lodge, which was redesigned by Flitcroft in 1745 for Sir Thomas Clarke, Master of the Rolls; the unpleasant Alexander Wedderburn (later the Earl of Rosslyn) lived here in the 1780s. In Frognal was Priory Lodge, where Dr Johnson stayed on occasions between 1748 and 1752.

*34. Heath House, 1910. From a watercolour by A. R. Quinton.*

35. Heathlands, the
house of Sir Francis
Willes, c.1800.

36. The Hill, the house
of Thomas Gattaker,
c.1800.

Frognal still contains several fine houses of the 18th century. No. 94, the Old Mansion is *c*.1700, Nos. 103–9 were built by Flitcroft *c*.1745 and he lived in No. 105. Nos. 108 and 110 are Queen Anne and Nos. 104 and 106 are dated *c*.1760.[17] On the summit of the Heath stands Heath House, built *c*.1744 when Christopher Arnold, goldsmith and active partner of Hoare's Bank,[18] took over two houses here and built the mansion later lived in by Samuel Hoare Snr. Behind Jack Straw's Castle cottages on land called, significantly, Littleworth, were swept away in order to build grander houses such as Heathlands, a mansion developed by Sir Francis Willes in the 1780s. Willes was a Decipherer, a confidential State post which he and his family monopolised for 125 years.[19] One Thomas Gattaker had a house nearby in the 1780s which was bought for Samuel Hoare Jnr. upon his marriage to Elizabeth Fry's sister in 1807, and where John Gurney Hoare, the best-known campaigner to save the Heath was born in 1810. This house, called The Hill, was bought and transformed by the owner of Sunlight Soap, William Lever, in 1906, and later owned by Lord Inverforth, the shipping magnate, in the 1920s.

Other large houses had been built near the Spaniards Inn. John Turner, a rich linendraper, built The Firs, shown in illustration 69, which has immense basements, and in front of which he planted the celebrated firs which were the inspiration of many illustrations and postcards. The house is now divided into separate dwellings. Parkgate, home of the parish church architect John Saunderson, straddled the parish boundary. The celebrated advocate Thomas Erskine (later lord Chancellor), moved here in *c*.1792[20] and remained until 1819, having constructed a tunnel beneath Spaniards Road to his extended garden on the other side of the road. His house is depicted in illustration 74.

[1] *The Journeys of Celia Fiennes*, ed. C. Morris, p. 121 (1949).
[2] George W. Potter, *Hampstead Wells*, p. 88 (1904).
[3] Foley House is not shown on the detailed 1762 map of Hampstead or on its terrier.
[4] *Gentleman's Magazine*, September 1731.
[5] George W. Potter, op. cit, p. 70
[6] Middlesex Sessions Records, 1710.
[7] Caroline A. White, *Sweet Hampstead*, p. 225 (1903).
[8] *Daily Post*, 17 June 1723.
[9] Anon., Local History Collection, London Borough of Camden.
[10] Hampstead Vestry minutes, 16 December 1791.
[11] Ibid, 22 June 1748.
[12] Ibid, 11 April 1839.
[13] See Geoffrey Harris, The Humanity of Hampstead Workhouse, *Camden History Review* No. 4.
[14] Hampstead Parish Church Trustees minutes, 22 October 1744.
[15] Middlesex Sessions Rolls, 1692. A Stephen Lobb of Hampstead was also granted a licence in 1691 but it is not clear if the same congregation was involved. See *Rosslyn Hill Chapel: A Short History 1692–1973*, p. 19 (1974).
[16] Felicity Marpole, 'A Romantic House in Hampstead' *Camden History Review*, No. 9.
[17] Christopher Wade, *The Streets of Hampstead*, p. 16 (1984).
[18] David Sullivan, article in *Hampstead and Highgate Express*, 25 May 1979.
[19] David Sullivan, ibid.
[20] Hampstead Rate Books.

# CHAPTER FOUR
# Developments in Corners

When the young John James Park finished the first history of Hampstead at the end of 1813 he could look from a rear window of his father's house at No. 18 Church Row and see almost nothing but fields. Finchley Road did not exist and nor, of course, did Fitzjohn's Avenue. The hamlet of West End was a pleasant walk away; past the old manor house at the corner of Frognal, Park could reach the Cock and Hoop inn at West End without passing another building. Looking south-east from the same window he could spy on Belsize House and on the 18th-century Rosslyn House in their secluded, landscaped gardens. From a front window he could see up the new burial ground to more fields stretching to Telegraph Hill. Beyond the houses of New End was the Heath, regarded not only for its beauty but for its yield of sand, gravel and wood.

Rivers were above ground still. Park, from the same rear window, could see a tributary of the Westbourne river where it rose in what today are the grounds of University College School in Frognal. At least seven tributaries of this river began in Hampstead, to meet by Kilburn Priory before it crossed beneath Kilburn High Road on its way to Hyde Park and beyond. This river, originally called the Kilburn this far up, is mentioned in a schoolboy's diary of 1826:

> Nov. 6: Mrs Jay came to tea. The children, Susan Yates and self went up the village to see the fire-works. Guy Fawkes day having been kept to-day as yesterday was Sunday. A sham battle was very well kept up by the boys who divided into two companies on either side of the Kil-bourne and assailed each other with squibs, crackers, etc.[1]

The Tyburn river, too, rose in Hampstead, one arm beginning at the junction of Fitzjohn's Avenue and Akenside Road by what was, in Park's time, the main public well, Shepherds Well; the other arm began in the grounds of Belsize House. The more important river, the Fleet, rose principally in two places – the Vale of Health and Kenwood, before it merged north of Camden Town and from there flowed to Blackfriars and the Thames. These two tributaries were the source of the Hampstead and Highgate ponds constructed as reservoirs in the 17th and 18th centuries by the Hampstead Water Company, or the Society of Hampstead Aqueducts as it was called on its formation in 1693, when William Paterson, one of the founders of the Bank of England, promoted it.

The main manor farm stretched uninterrupted from Park's back garden to St John's Wood, and also over to Kilburn Lane which is now the southern arm of West End Lane. Further farmland lay between the lane and Kilburn High

37. *The Cock and Hoop, West End Lane, just before its demolition in 1900.*

Road. This peaceful, visual and physical connection between the village and West End is the most difficult to envisage today, given that the Finchley Road now bisects the old farm as completely as it does the imagination and the sensibilities. Also, the houses mask the slope which stretches west from the parish church whose bell, no doubt, woke Park each morning and whose sound could be heard in the comfortable villas of West End.

The Finchley Road derived from the need of a Colonel Eyre to open up his St John's Wood estate. In 1819 he proposed roads which, from about Acacia Road, went north-west to Kilburn High Road and north-east to Belsize Lane with an extension roughly on the line of the later Fitzjohn's Avenue. This provoked opposition from the lord of the manor, Sir Thomas Maryon Wilson Snr., from the residents of Belsize Lane, and presumably the tradesmen and innkeepers of Rosslyn Hill and the High Street were not too happy that the route avoided their establishments. One reason advanced against the proposal was that the road to Belsize Lane would spoil a Hampstead whose description most estate agents would covet:

Hampstead is a very eligible situation from its nearness to the metropolis. It has enough publicity at present. It is desirable, in order to meet the taste and choice of the Residents there for privacy, not to put in practice any measure to make it more public. The Gentlemen there who fill official situations, or are in professions, or are Merchants of the first rank in the Metropolis, wish to preserve about their Dwellings the quiet and privacy which the Country should secure for their refreshment and necessary retirement from active duties and pursuits daily prosecuted in the Metropolis.[2]

48

From this it appears that the lord of the manor did, indeed, care for the seclusion and peace of Hampstead for, in theory, what opened up Colonel Eyre's estate also made Hampstead ripe for profitable development. He died soon after this proposal was beaten off and he left his Hampstead estate to his son, Sir Thomas Jnr., under conditions which helped to preserve the area's seclusion for a long time.[3]

Other evidence against the proposal describes the mobility, or otherwise, of Hampstead residents:

> Not one in twenty of the Gentlemen in Hampstead would have any occasion for professional pursuits or objects of business to go along the proposed road; their business or concerns lie in the City or about the Inns of Court, and not westwards of Tottenham Court road . . . The tradesmen of Hampstead of every description draw their goods and commodities from those parts of the Metropolis which the present roads to Hampstead are most convenient for them to be drawn by . . . Some few of the families resident in Hampstead do occasionally in the season go to Brighton or other places next the sea, but would not pass along the proposed road.[4]

In 1824 Colonel Eyre introduced a new plan – a turnpike road which went from St John's Wood to Finchley. Sir Thomas Jnr. opposed this as well, as did the Hampstead Vestry, although with a 14–11 vote against, with six abstentions, they were far from adamant about it.[5] The line of the road went through the manor farm and Sir Thomas infuriated his affluent tenants at West End by suggesting, instead, a diversion which went westwards just above St John's Wood and used West End Lane as the main road north. This, of course, ensured that the West End residents supported Eyre's scheme.[6]

Parliament agreed to the Eyre route and Sir Thomas, once the advocate of farmland surrounding the gentlemen's retreats of Hampstead, obliged the turnpike trustees to pay building-land prices in compensation for his lost land.[7] Ironically, the frontages of Finchley Road on his estate were not built on in his lifetime.

As this was happening development in the main town leapfrogged over several fields to increase the population near Pond Street. Pond Street was an old quarter, and a name first encountered in 1609.[8] The pond was on the site of the present bus terminus until 1835 by which time it was unhealthy and unpleasant. The residents of the area drew their water from the Shepherd's Well (at the junction of today's Akenside Road and Fitzjohn's Avenue) through pipes and by gravity. In 1807 the Pond Street residents protested that the supply of water had ceased. The pipes ran across the grounds of Rosslyn House and Robert Milligan, then the tenant, contended that the fault was in the supply rather than the pipes which he was bound to maintain. With the Vestry's approval he offered to remove the old pipes and construct a new footpath to the well from Rosslyn Hill to replace an earlier footpath across his estate.[9] Herein lies the probable origin of the mysterious Shepherd's Walk which runs through to Rosslyn Hill from Fitzjohn's Avenue; another alley nearby, called Shepherd's Path, comes to a full stop after a few yards at the boundary of the old Rosslyn House estate and this is probably the only part remaining of the older footpath.

A remnant of village green still survives by St Stephen's church on Haverstock Hill; the green once included the site of the church and its hall, and ran along Pond Street in a strip towards South End Green. By 1762 there were at

*38. South End Green, then known as Pond Street. Publ. c.1828.*

*39. Shepherd's Well. Engraving publ. in Hone's* Table Book *1827.*

40. *Downshire Hill.
Publ. 1842.*

least 39 dwellings scattered in the street and around South End Green.[10] These included the White Horse public house, mentioned as early as 1721. Adjacent, virtually on the bank of the river Fleet, was a brewery established by 1750 by Michael Combrune, a London brewer. He owned, or supplied, five establishments in Hampstead including the Bull and Bush and the Nag's Head. One house in the area was occupied by the Venetian ambassador in 1774.[11] On the site of No. 31 Pond Street was the house of Thomas Rumsey, whose bequest provided coal at Christmas-time for poor people.[12]

The new development in this area was at Downshire Hill and Keats Grove – the latter formerly called John Street. It began *c*.1814 with leases contrived by the lord of the manor to be attractive.[13] If he had lived longer or had not chosen to restrict his heir so closely, then the Downshire Hill type of development might well have extended up the hill to the village. The developer of these 14 acres was William Coleman, an auctioneer of Curzon Street, Mayfair; he also joined with Edward Carlile the following year in buying up the estate which contained the Rosslyn Hill Chapel and the large property subsequently known as Carlile House. This was not the only business deal between Coleman and Carlile, for in 1817 the former surrendered his interest in the site of St John's chapel in Downshire Hill to James Curry, a cleric, William Woods, a builder, and Edward Carlile.[14] It is possible that Woods, who was also a brickmaker, based off the Strand and in Lambeth, also built Downshire Hill as well as the chapel.

It was probably intended that the chapel should become an adjunct to St John's in Church Row, hence the same dedication. It became, instead, a proprietary chapel, supported by the funds of the minister and its congregation, a common enough occurrence in the days when there were more would-be preachers than there were official churches to support them. St

John's, Downshire Hill, opened in 1823, is now the last of its kind in London.

Across the road, as an added attraction, the Freemasons Arms was opened in 1819; its grounds included, until recently, the last pell-mell court in Britain.

Downshire Hill joined Willow Road, as yet unnamed, for the willows had yet to come in 1845. The upper part of Willow Road was laid out across the open Heath in 1785 by Henry White, a builder.[15] Ironically, White is regarded as the first hero of the long fight to save the Heath from encroachment, but his concern for preservation appears to have gone no further than his own pocket.

An oddly isolated development occurred at the same time in Kilburn. Fulke Greville Howard bought the Kilburn Priory estate from Richard Marsh in 1819. Howard may well have hoped that the publicised expansion of the Eyre estate in St John's Wood would soon reach his land, but in this he was optimistic. At any rate, Howard began development, without using his own capital, and the principal buildings erected were seven villas in Greville Place, built at right-angles to the main road as though promising an extension. These were built in the early 1820s but nothing else happened until the 1840s.

The builder of this group of houses was a surveyor called George Pocock whose family life was unexpectedly revealed in a diary, lately rediscovered and published, written by his young son John Thomas Pocock. Some of the family were extensive builders in Islington and elsewhere. George made some profit on Greville Place, but not much, as he was arrested for debt in 1826 and imprisoned in the King's Bench Prison, to where his son used to walk the eight miles to see him – a distance quite short in the life of young Pocock, who regularly strode 25 miles in a day. George Pocock died in 1829, his last days movingly described by his 15-year-old son in his diary:

> My Father much worse to-day and sensible of approaching dissolution. In the afternoon he called us all in the room and bid us farewell individually. There were some of his favourite russet pippins on the table, and he divided them, giving half an apple to each child; this, he adopted as a relief to the solemn scene. My Father was a strong minded man. I never knew him to be overcome by his feelings until now, but this affecting scene was too much for him. He thought he would have gone through it with fortitude, but when it came to the eldest children, Emily and myself, for our share, he could not longer conceal his grief. Nature had her way and my father, covering his eyes with shrunken hands, wept, bitterly wept and we were equally moved. To me – and me only – he gave a whole apple, and this I will keep for ever.[16]

The hamlet of 'le Westende', as it was described in 1535, was sparsely developed. It was peaceful enough for the residents not only to hear the parish church bell in the village but, in the 19th century, to hear Big Ben as well. The village green, hemmed in by roads, remains – it was rescued from a building scheme in the 19th century. On the green the short-lived West End fair took place in July each year, until the magistrates suppressed it after particularly unruly scenes in 1819. The fair was of no antiquity, had no legal status and changed from a harmless community fair for the sale of gingerbread and such like to one which the Vestry minutes describe as a scene of 'drunkenness, debauchery and the practice of every species of vice and immorality'.[17]

There were two pockets of houses at North End connected by the track

across the Sandy Heath. One area contained the old Wyldes farmhouse and two taverns. The Wyldes estate, as previously mentioned[18], was part of the Eton College holding in Hampstead. The first recorded tenant, John Slanning, was arraigned in 1556 for felling an excessive number of trees both here and in Kenwood, when the London demand for timber was tempting. The original farmhouse was probably built in the 1590s and it now makes up the main section of the present structure called Old Wyldes. By 1744 a large barn had been erected next to the house – this is now called Wyldes. In the early 19th century North End was in demand for summer lets, and it was to Wyldes that John Linnell, the landscape painter, came and eventually settled. Nearby was a house variously called North End Place, Wildwood or Pitt House, the latter name from the reclusive stay, in 1767, of the then Prime Minister, William Pitt the Elder. This Hampstead convalescence, while Pitt struggled to recover from a mental breakdown, was contrived by the owner of the house, Charles Dingley, who had political ambitions of his own until an injury sustained at the hustings of 1769 ended his life. The house was demolished in 1952.

Of the two taverns here, the Bull and Bush was here by 1721 and the Hare and Hounds thirty years later.

On the London side of the Spaniards Road the swampy valley called Hatches Bottom (from its tenant Samuel Hatch), was drained by the Hampstead Water Company in 1777. As it was still the least desirable place in the parish the poor-houses were transferred here, and the village pound, which had previously been near Jack Straw's Castle, was moved to just above the valley. In the pound were incarcerated stray animals taken in by the Heath keeper, who exacted a fine for their recovery. The first mention of the name

*41. A view on Hampstead Heath, looking towards London, from a drawing by F. J. Sarjent, 1804. The Vale of Health is in the foreground.*

53

'Vale of Health' for this area occurs in a will of 1801.[19] There is no basis for the legendary explanations that the name was acquired when it became a refuge during the Great Plague of 1665, or because it was used for washing by laundresses. The name was almost certainly coined by a person anxious to attract new tenants to the place once it had been drained; the ruse was sufficiently successful by 1814 for the authorities to be considering a further move of the paupers, presumably because their presence was then an embarrassment. In 1815 the first notable resident, the poet Leigh Hunt, came here and from this time the social tone of the Vale changed.

[1] John Thomas Pocock, *The Diary of a London Schoolboy 1826–1830* (1980) (Camden History Society).

[2] Petition of Sir Thomas Maryon Wilson against the proposal, quoted in Professor F. M. L. Thompson, op. cit., p. 115.

[3] See Chapter 6.

[4] Evidence of George Paxon. Professor F. M. L. Thompson, op. cit., p. 117.

[5] Hampstead Vestry minutes, 24 March 1824.

[6] Professor F. M. L. Thompson, op. cit., p. 122.

[7] Ibid, p. 123.

[8] Hampstead Manor Court Rolls 1609.

[9] Hampstead Vestry minutes, 19 April 1808.

[10] James Ellis, 1762 map of Hampstead.

[11] Hampstead Rate Books, 1774.

[12] See p. 38.

[13] Professor F. M. L. Thompson, op. cit., p. 125.

[14] Anon., *A Short History of St John's Downshire Hill, Hampstead*, p. 6 (1973?).

[15] Hampstead Manor Court Rolls, 9 May 1785.

[16] John Thomas Pocock, op. cit., p. 61.

[17] Hampstead Vestry minutes, 13 August 1819.

[18] See p. 12.

[19] Helen C. Bentwich, *The Vale of Health on Hampstead Heath*, p. 24 (1968). Repr. by Carlile House Press, 1977.

CHAPTER FIVE

# Explosion of Directions

Until 1855 the Vestry had a restricted ability to govern. Its earlier minutes reveal scant attention to the growth in the number of houses, save a lament that a great many were unrated, and little concern that poverty, even in Hampstead, was worsening. Of course, only decisions feature in minutes – observations and opinions do not, and we can only assume that some residents were making efforts and noises to remedy the most glaring deficiencies in the Vestry's powers.

In the matter of poor relief, for example, the Vestry helped only when the person became a pauper, with the subsequent loss of liberty and rights in the workhouse which ranged from a restriction on movement to the legalised use of one's body after death for dissection in the anatomy schools. There was, however, a class of person on a low income who still retained a roof over their heads, but who could be forced into the workhouse by a prolonged illness. It was for this group that the Hampstead Parochial Benefit Society was formed by William Bleamire, a magistrate, in 1781; members paid a monthly sum which entitled them to sickness pay and a small pension for their old age.

Common in the late 18th and early 19th centuries was the dispensary, an establishment supported by the better-off in the town; they were able, according to the amount of their subscription, to nominate poorer people for medical treatment. Highgate had such a dispensary by 1787 but Hampstead residents were slow in establishing their own. At the instigation of one of Hampstead's energetic vicars, the Rev. Thomas Ainger, the Hampstead Self-Supporting Dispensary opened its doors at a house at No. 10 New End, next to the workhouse, in 1846. In 1853 the Hampstead Provident Dispensary, as it was then called, acquired its own building at No. 16, and on this occasion the lord of the manor, Sir Thomas Maryon Wilson, who was at odds with both Vestry and residents over the matter of the Heath, provided the bricks at cost. We do not know whether his motives were generous or propritiatory. The soup kitchen which sold soup at a penny a quart in the winter months from c.1844 transferred from the workhouse to the new Dispensary. This institution survived until the 1911 National Insurance legislation made it superfluous, but the rooms were still let out until its demolition in 1949.

As for the unfortunate inmates of the workhouse, one may imagine their existence from some lines written much later, in 1890: 'The inmates are kindly treated, but any one who is refractory and who does not at once yield to remonstrance, is punished, either by separation, the loss of the occasional privilege of taking a walk beyond the workhouse grounds or in some other way.'[1]

PROPOSED DISPENSARY
AND SOUP KITCHEN,
NEW END,
HAMPSTEAD.

*42. The proposed
Dispensary and Soup
Kitchen, New End.
From an appeal
brochure c.1852.*

In 1825 the Vestry was involved in a scheme which artificially created jobs
by using pauper labour to dig and construct a pond on the Heath. This is
usually thought to have been the Leg of Mutton Pond (a name derived from
its shape) on West Heath, but the recent excavations there have revealed that
the pond is a natural one with sloping banks all round.[2] Wherever the work
took place, it seems to have been an embellishment for which the Vestry was
derided and criticised.

A benefit society, of sorts, began in 1781 when 'certain well-disposed
Hampstead gentlemen' formed a club called the Philo-Investigists, the rules
of which pompously forbade anything but very temperate conversation at its
gatherings. To compound the oddness of its name, the Club's president was a
Mr Eagle Caswell. From the names and known residences of its most prominent members it is safe to assume that this was a tradesmen's club. In 1787 the
Society began a Sunday School which soon boasted 120 pupils and the

patronage of Edward Montagu, the eminent lawyer, who lived in Flitcroft's old house in Frognal. It was then decided to choose twelve boys and twelve girls from the Sunday scholars for daily instruction by Thomas Mitchell, who had not only kept a private school in Flask Walk from 1778 but was secretary of the Society. The number of pupils of what became the Hampstead Parochial School increased, Mitchell's son took over the duties on his father's death in 1799, but from 1806 the school led a precarious existence until it was housed in a new building in Holly Bush Vale. Here, children were admitted as early as two years of age, paying 2d per week.

Schooling for the poor children outside the workhouse was beyond the powers of the Vestry. For these children the National Schools for the Education of the Poor in the Principles of the Established Church were established, generally attached to churches such as Christ Church, in 1856. The Hampstead Parochial School also came under the aegis of the National Society, which may explain why it survived when the Philo-Investigists did not.

Church building began in earnest in the 1850s as the old estates of Hampstead were broken up and present-day Hampstead constructed. It was sometimes as important to have a respectable place of worship on a new development as it is today to be near an Underground station.

The three earliest churches, the parish church, the Well Walk chapel and the St John's chapel in Downshire Hill, have already been mentioned. Two early 19th-century churches should also be noted. The first is St Mary's Roman Catholic chapel in Holly Place, and the second is the Baptist chapel originally at Holly Mount. The congregation of St Mary's was established when the Abbé Morel, a French refugee, held Catholic services in Oriel House, a building near Church Row which was demolished in the 1880s. In 1816, thirteen years before the Catholic Emancipation Act, the discreet Catholic church was built in Holly Place, very plain and unadorned at the time. A contemporary diary[3] shows that before Oriel House the local Catholics celebrated Mass at a house belonging to a Lucy Nihill – the ratebooks show her at Heathfield (now Ladywell Court) in East Heath Road, and later at Rosslyn Lodge in Lyndhurst Road in the period 1784–92.

The Baptists are known to have begun meeting in Hampstead in 1818[4] at 17 Holly Mount. However, in the ratebooks for 1774 to 1796 there is a reference to a 'cellar under the Tabernacle' in relation to a ratepayer with premises roughly on the site of today's Underground station in Heath Street. It need not, of course, have been a chapel at all – it may have been an old alehouse, but it could indicate an earlier presence of the Baptists in Hampstead.

A division of the Baptists in Hampstead occurred in 1825 when the Strict Baptists removed from Holly Mount to a new chapel in New End, but the old congregation appears to have been the basis for the regulars in the overbearing church in Heath Street designed by C. G. Searle in 1861. The greater part of the cost of this building was borne by a London merchant, James Harvey, as a sign of gratitude that the Hampstead air had revived the health of his ailing son. Church architecture more sensitive to the scale of Heath Street may be seen further up the hill in the Friends' Meeting House, designed by Fred Rowntree in 1907.

An unusual hexagonal building was constructed by Alfred Waterhouse for

43. *St Mary's church,*
*Holly Place.*

the Congregationalists in 1884 at the corner of Lyndhurst Road and Rosslyn Hill. This church was once sufficiently active to have a mission hall in west Kentish Town but it has now been unused for years and is being converted into housing and a small arts' centre.

The only new Church of England building in the centre of town was Christ Church, built in 1852; it took up part of Hampstead Square and obliterated the Victoria Tea Gardens. It was designed by Samuel Dawkes with substantial alterations since by George Gilbert Scott the younger and Ewan Christian. The congregation for this church came partly from the Well Walk chapel, but its establishment was a facet of the continuing battle between the lord of the manor, Sir Thomas Maryon Wilson, and his opponents in the battle to save the Heath and the East Park estate from development. Sir Thomas had the gift

*44. Old houses and the Friends' Meeting House, Heath Street, 1911. From a drawing by A. R. Quinton, reproduced from* Barratt's Annals of Hampstead *(1912).*

of the living of the parish church. This was not, it has to be said, a valuable one since the vicar had long ago lost the tithes, but the parish church still had prestige and influence and the vicar was in Sir Thomas's pocket. His opponents, in seeking to dilute his power, proposed a church uncomfortably close to the parish church instead of within the new residential areas springing up; their application was granted and a large and valuable part of the parish church territory was allotted to Christ Church.[5]

Christ Church was built in time for the heyday of church attendance. In 1886, 2325 people attended on one Sunday.[6] Let us hope that it was less class-conscious than the parish church where tradesmen were expected to occupy the galleries and not the downstairs pews.

After Christ Church opened the vacant Well Walk chapel was taken by a Presbyterian congregation which had previously been in Perrins Court in a building later occupied by the *Hampstead and Highgate Express*. (These Presbyterians are not to be confused with those already at Rosslyn Hill Chapel and who later became Unitarians. Confusingly, the Well Walk Presbyterians built themselves the Trinity Chapel in 1862, only a few doors from the rebuilt Rosslyn Hill Chapel.)

Once the worshippers had departed from Well Walk the Hampstead Volunteers moved in. In 1798 the towns of England were aroused by a call to arms: England was at war with France and there was rebellion in Ireland. Voluntary battalions were raised everywhere to prepare for a feared invasion, though in the event they saw no active service. Josiah Boydell, renowned engraver, wealthy and energetic resident of West End, instigated the formation of the Loyal Hampstead Association, of which he was commander.[7] This disbanded, with the Peace of Amiens, in 1802, but Boydell reformed it as the Hampstead Loyal Volunteers the following year when war with France

*45. Inspection of the East Middlesex Militia, Well Walk. From the* Illustrated London News, *Jan. 20, 1855.*

was renewed and a wave of patriotism again swept through the land. At a meeting on the Heath that year 700 men were sworn in after being assured by Boydell that, contrary to ugly rumour, they were not being conscripted into the regular army. The officers of this new association included Thomas Norton Longman, the publisher, Dobson Willoughby Esquire, who lived in the High Street and after whose family Willoughby Road is named, James Poulter, grocer of both Hampstead and Highgate, and Charles Holford, whose family lent its name to every good cause. The effectiveness of this mixture of gentry and tradesmen under attack was never put to the test, but when the successors of the Volunteers took over the Well Walk Chapel in 1862 William Bodkin, a local magistrate, recalled that in 1811 when they were at target practice on the Heath, only one man hit the centre bull all day and he was seen to close his eyes as he fired.[8] In 1880 this force became part of a new 3rd Middlesex Rifle Volunteer corps and a public subscription helped to build them a new Drill Hall at Holly Bush Vale which is now used by the Everyman Cinema. The Volunteers were, in modern parlance, a Home Guard. The equivalent of today's Territorials were the Royal East Middlesex Militia who built two unsightly wings jutting from the front of Burgh House for their training purposes, and in 1863 erected barracks in Willow Road which have since been converted into local authority housing.

The chief officers of Mr Boydell's original patriotic force were Charles

Holford and Conrad Smalley. All three men were also members of the Hampstead Dinner Club, an association of the town's principal residents which began in 1784. Probably the real influence in the town was exercised not at the infrequently convened meetings of local tradesmen in the shape of the Vestry, but here at this monthly club where the occupants of some of the grander houses consumed turtle, venison and champagne.

*46. Burgh House c.1870, when it was the headquarters of the East Middlesex Militia. The buildings in the foreground have since been demolished.*

The members of the Dinner Club, which lasted until 1859, lent their names to a number of Hampstead causes, but they were the entrenched, paternalistic, Church of England segment of the community. It was left to the mainly low-church and literary residents to form what was to be an important feature of Hampstead's cultural development, the Hampstead Subscription Library, in 1833. The original committee was sprinkled with Unitarians and was supported by progressive publishers such as Charles Knight whose magazine, *The Penny Cyclopaedia*, brought knowledge to the scarcely literate and near-bankruptcy to its proprietor. John Constable was a life shareholder and publishers such as Longman, Bell and John Murray, all local residents, donated books. The Library opened at what is now No. 65 Flask Walk and moved twice in its early, erratic, history before settling in 1884 at Stanfield House in the High Street (Nos. 85–8). It closed, finally, in 1966.

When the second Long Room and the ballroom became private residences, Hampstead was without a public meeting-place of any size. It was decided to create some Assembly Rooms and to this end a trust bought Romney's old studio on Holly Bush Hill and engaged a publican to convert the adjoining stables into the Holly Bush Tavern in 1807. Finance to enlarge and convert the premises was raised by the unusual device of a tontine lottery, whereby people were invited to subscribe on the understanding that the last of them alive would be the main beneficiary – grounds, surely, for an Agatha Christie thriller. These rooms were made redundant when the Vestry Hall was opened in 1878 and ten years later the Hampstead Constitutional Club, a name disguising the Conservative Party at play, were tenants until Clough Williams Ellis, the architect of Portmeirion, converted the building back into a private house.

By mid-century the days of 'Hampstead in Middlesex' were fading and 'Hampstead in London' had become inevitable.[9] In the metropolis administration at vestry level was confused. At random, throughout London, such things as roads, lighting and poor relief were the responsibility of numerous self-elected bodies. Water supplies were a matter of private enterprise. The New River Company extended its pipes from Highgate to Hampstead in 1853,

*47. Josiah Boydell. Engraved by R. W. Satchwell.*

but there is no record of Vestry encouragement to do so. Gas suppliers in London parcelled out the capital, much to the fury of the vestries, which were more concerned to have price competition than to avoid the nuisance of duplicated pipes beneath the pavements. In Hampstead, where there were insufficient houses to attract early competition, the Imperial Gas Company was given permission to lay pipes in 1823 and thereafter held the monopoly.

Speculators, running up terraces across the fields, were free of planning restrictions or checks on the sanitary amenities provided; the owners of the unhygienic older properties were not obliged to improve them. Many vestrymen were also builders or small-time landlords themselves, and the last thing they wanted was supervision in such matters. Their interests, instead, were served by the continued weakness of the vestries and, as a result, meetings of open vestries were trifling, repetitive affairs. In Hampstead large attendances occurred only if there was some encroachment on a footpath or if there was a prospect of expenditure which would increase the level of parish expenditure. 'Liberty and the avoidance of expense ran religion close in popularity.'[10]

Exploiting this chaos the railway companies, with allies and shareholders in Parliament, ran their lines through residential areas or across commons with something like impunity. In St Pancras parish, which bore the brunt of the railway-building age, the Vestry was concerned at the loss of rate revenue

*48. Hampstead Subscription Library at Stanfield House in the High Street. Photograph 1910.*

when streets were demolished rather than at any social consequences.

There *was* no overall London authority. Even the conservative J. Toulmin Smith declared in 1852 that 'the present condition of this huge metropolis exhibits the most extraordinary anomaly in England. Abounding in wealth and in intelligence, by far the greater part of it is yet absolutely without any municipal government whatever.'[11] The City of London successfully fought the introduction of a metropolitan body with a blatant regard for its own privileges and a disregard for the needs of the rest of London; the City excluded itself from the Metropolitan Police Act of 1830 and ran its own force. When the Metropolitan Board of Works was eventually established in 1855 the City escaped its authority. Some London vestries were content to connive in this for they feared the expense that reform would bring, and the loss of autonomy. The ill-judged grouping of Poor Law bodies in 1837 to form unions of parishes had left a bad taste, for then the parishes had lost the right, but not the expense, of looking after their own poor. Hampstead relinquished power to the Edmonton Union but regained it again in 1848, when it became the grateful beneficiary of a new workhouse at New End (1845) in which the Vestry could have an office and meeting room and again manage to delay the building of a vestry hall.

*Opposite:*
*49. Finchley Road baths, 1888.*

Typically (for the treatment of London government by Parliament is not an attractive story at any period), the Metropolitan Board of Works, the first governors of extended London, came about not because Parliament had imagination but because of a succession of cholera epidemics in the capital, notably those of 1832, 1849 and 1854. It was imperative that something be done about the sewer system and for this the MBW was primarily set up. Typically, too, its designated geographical area had more to do with history than with pragmatic considerations – populous areas such as West Ham were excluded simply because they were not in the area covered by the old Bills of Mortality for London.

The MBW was not a popular body; its good works in drainage, its construction of the Embankment, its creation of new streets through old slums, were obscured by long-running scandals of corruption. It was not popularly elected either, consisting mainly of vestry nominations. The vestries were reformed into elected assemblies at the same time as the MBW was established but they had a very narrow electoral base; voters were those who occupied houses rated at £40 per annum and over, which, in Hampstead, provided an electorate of about 1000 males. It is doubtful if the Vestry changed much in make-up at this stage – more radical movement occurred in 1874 when election took place by wards and necessarily brought in people from outside the old town centre.

One statutory responsibility of the new Hampstead Vestry was the appointment of a Medical Officer of Health, who had a salary of £50 per annum. The Vestry was fortunate in its first appointment. Dr Charles Lord was a zealous reformer in the matter of public health and he and his colleague in St Pancras both made themselves unpopular with vested and vestry interests by campaigning for the removal of cowsheds and slaughterhouses from the metropolis.[12] Dr Lord was, however, unable to persuade the Vestry to erect baths and washhouses during his term of office, or to erase the slum

called Crockett's Court which stood at the top of the High Street – the 1851 census shows 117 people living in its 18 dwellings.

The first baths and washhouses were provided by charity and not by the Vestry. The combined Wells and Campden charities, now replete with funds from their developed lands, provided the amenity, for once in the Kilburn part of the borough, in Palmerston Road. These were opened in 1887. The following year the charity opened a second baths in Flask Walk, in a building designed by Henry Legg, which closed in 1978 and has more recently been converted into housing. The third baths and washhouses were erected by the Vestry, also in 1888, in Finchley Road in place of the Swiss Cottage Skating Rink; this was superseded by the modern Swiss Cottage baths and a branch of Sainsbury's is now on the site.

Cholera was not the only health worry in London: smallpox was another. The Metropolitan Asylums Board, set up by the government to amend the uneven or inadequate provision of hospitals in London, chose a site at Hampstead called Bartrams, which consisted of adjacent fields at the rear of some substantial houses fronting Hampstead Green, and backing on to what is now Lawn Road. Here, despite protests, the Board erected some sheds in 1869 to cope with epidemics of fever but when, the following year, smallpox swept through the metropolis, Bartrams was suddenly crowded with additional sheds as patients arrived from all over north London. Uproar ensued in Hampstead and neighbouring St Pancras, for it was claimed by the residents that the loosely supervised hospital was spreading the disease into the locality. They were to be proved right. Maps later showed how smallpox was prevalent in the area of Fleet Road and, incidentally, near the smallpox hospital at Highgate. Closed in 1872, the smallpox wards were reopened in 1876 – again there was a local outbreak of the disease. A protracted campaign led to their closure again in 1882. Some amusement was caused when Sir William Wyatt, a member of the Metropolitan Asylums Board who had stoutly defended the placing of the hospital in Hampstead and scorned the fears of residents, was himself a leading opponent in 1881 of the plan by St Pancras Vestry to erect a contagious diseases hospital at Finchley close to his own property.[13]

The North West Fever Hospital was then built on the Bartrams, taking up the site of the house previously owned by the Post Office reformer, Sir Rowland Hill. In 1884 they were obliged to send any smallpox patient to the quarantine long boats on the Thames. Later another large house on the Green called Tensleys, the former home of Sir Francis Palgrave (father of the *Golden Treasury* compiler), was demolished to make way for the Hampstead General Hospital, and these two establishments were later absorbed into the Royal Free Hospital.

A new ally had, by then, appeared in Hampstead to assist residents in repelling hospitals or builders on the Heath. This was the first local newspaper, the *Hampstead and Highgate Express*, begun by an unknown proprietor in October 1860 and printed in 1861 in the disused Baptist chapel at No. 17 Holly Mount. In 1862 it was bought by its most famous owner, George Samuel Jealous, a City printer and Liberal philanthropist. Jealous lived in the Vale of Health, where he encouraged a young neighbour of his, the future Lord Northcliffe, to visit the newspaper on press days. He also gave him a small

*Opposite:*
*50. The proposed site of the Hampstead Fever Hospital showing the sheds which housed the smallpox patients.*

*51. An interior view of the Hampstead Smallpox Hospital. From the* Illustrated London News, *Oct. 7, 1871.*

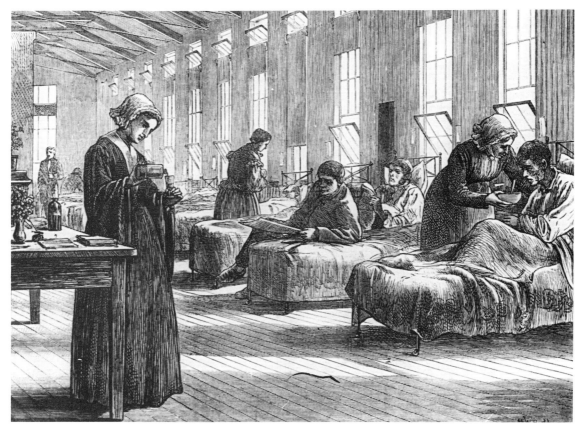

printing set as a birthday present. The family retained the paper after his death in 1896 until the 2nd World War.

Its rival was the *Hampstead News*, a paper which had its origins in an early free sheet called the *South Hampstead Advertiser*, printed in Fairfax Road from December 1880. In the 1950s it and its proprietors, Messrs Baines and Scarsbrook, were sold to the owners of the *Hornsey Journal*, and the contract to print the programmes for the Henry Wood Promenade Concerts, held almost since their inception, went with them.

Almost as old as the *Express* is the *Kilburn Times*, first issued in March 1868 by Rowland George Bassett of Carlton Road, Kilburn.

One municipal improvement, welcomed by everyone, was the opening of a new cemetery at Fortune Green in 1876. It is one of the more attractive municipal burial grounds, the product of a lavish beginning – it had, originally, a staff of thirty gardeners. It contains two remarkable memorials, one in the shape of a massive church organ for Charles Barritt, and a large *art deco* design for a Mr Bianchi. Also buried here are Marie Lloyd, Dennis Brain, Nigel Balchin, Kate Greenaway and Lord Lister.

Without collusion a number of important public buildings were erected down the hill towards Belsize Park in the latter part of the 19th century, as though to signal a reorientation of the town. This was not surprising given that the terrain of the village was difficult and overcrowded, and the western part of the parish, through which Fitzjohn's Avenue now runs, was still agricultural.

First there was St Stephen's church at the junction with Pond Street. This bulky Gothic building by S. S. Teulon, which has some admirers, was consecrated on the last day of 1869. Its first vicar came from the proprietary chapel of St John in Downshire Hill and it was anticipated that his congregation would follow him, rendering the old chapel unnecessary. This did not happen, and it is ironic that St Stephen's has now stood empty and dangerous for some years, waiting for expensive conversion or demolition, while St John's still gathers the faithful into its classical portals.

Then there was the police station. The Metropolitan force was first housed in 1830 in small premises at No. 9 Holly Place – a plaque marks the house. Four years later it moved to the junction of Holly Hill and Heath Street – opposite today's Underground station – and then in 1870 a new station was opened in Rosslyn Hill on the site of the old Red Lion public house, nearly opposite the present police station which was built in 1913.

Then, at last, the Vestry built its own premises, in Haverstock Hill; they were opened in April 1878 on the site of a large mansion called Hillfield. This was made necessary by the need to accommodate the newly enlarged Vestry and was not motivated by a wish to expand its services to the community.[14] The siting of the Hall to the south of the old town was not popular with the traders and, as Professor Thompson points out, with development already begun on the open fields around Fitzjohn's Avenue, the Vestry should have delayed a few years and chosen instead the inevitable location of Swiss Cottage. When that location was decided upon in the 1950s the borough was overtaken by the event of the merger into Camden and a new town hall was never built.

52. *Entrance to
Hampstead Cemetery,
Fortune Green. From*
The Builder, *Nov.
25, 1876.*

53. *Hampstead Town
Hall. Postcard c.1905.*

The design of the Vestry Hall by H. E. Kendall the District Surveyor, and his partner Frederick Mew, is witheringly described by Pevsner as 'Crushingly mean; a disgrace to so prosperous and artistic a borough',[15] but although there were reservations about the interior quality of the building, most people would probably think that Pevsner's verdict is itself a bit mean.

On the other hand, the fire services reversed the trend to the south for a time. In the 18th century Hampstead's two engines were reported to be out of repair[16] and were then housed at the King's Arms in the High Street. Nothing further is heard of them until a new engine was bought in 1837. In 1869 the Metropolitan Fire Brigade, now responsible for the Hampstead area, converted a house called Belle Vue, opposite the Vestry Hall site in Haverstock Hill, into a fire station. Here they remained until the police had moved down to Rosslyn Hill, and the fire brigade then took the corner site opposite the Hampstead Underground station: their new building was probably designed by Alfred Mott of the Metropolitan Board of Works. This closed in 1915 when the brigade moved to Lancaster Grove.

[1] Frederic Hill in *The Records of the Manor, Parish and Borough of Hampstead*, ed. F. E. Baines (1890).
[2] Information ex Margaret Maher, 1985.
[3] *The Mawhood Diary (1764–90)*, ed. E. E. Reynolds. Catholic Record Society, Vol. 50. See also article by Dominic Bellenger in *Camden History Review*, No. 10.
[4] *Baptist Quarterly*, Vol. 36, No. 3, July 1975.
[5] See Professor F. M. L. Thompson, op. cit., p. 384.
[6] Christopher Wade, *The Streets of Hampstead*, op. cit., p. 44.
[7] See article in *Hampstead Annual 1905–6* and relics housed in the Local History Library, London Borough of Camden.
[8] George W. Potter, op. cit., p. 92.
[9] This occurred, officially, at the formation of the London County Council in 1889.
[10] Professor F. M. L. Thompson, op. cit., p. 391.
[11] J. Toulmin Smith, *The Metropolis and its Municipal Administration*, p. 7.
[12] See *Reminiscences of Mr Charles Lord 1889* (Local History Library, London Borough of Camden) and article by Dr Barbara Ely, 'Till Death through Ripe Old Age', in *Camden History Review*, No. 3.
[13] *Hampstead and Highgate Express*, 21 May 1881.
[14] Professor F. M. L. Thompson, op. cit., p. 407.
[15] Nikolaus Pevsner, *London, Except the Cities of London and Westminster* (the *Buildings of England* series), p. 189 (1952).
[16] Hampstead Vestry minutes 27 June 1753.

# CHAPTER SIX

# Spaces Kept Open

In 1824 Sir Thomas Maryon Wilson Jnr., lord of the Hampstead manor, opposed the projected line of the Finchley Road across his fields. It was the intention of his late father's will, he testified, that his Hampstead property should remain as it was, although his heir had permission to grant building leases on his lands at Woolwich and Charlton. The later campaigners to save the Heath seem not to have known of this statement, but its content was the basis for the protracted battle and their eventual victory.

The Maryon Wilson estate in Hampstead consisted of 356 acres of farmland to the west and north-west of the village, on either side of the Finchley Road, and 60 acres called the East Park estate sandwiched between the eastern part of the Heath and Parliament Hill Fields and Kenwood. The lord also had manorial rights over the East, West and Sandy Heaths. The position was that he owned the Heaths subject to the rights and uses of adjoining copyholders which were determined by manor custom, and which were similar to those found elsewhere in the country. This (almost tacit) relationship between manorial lord and tenant copyholder had not yet been properly defined in the courts. In any case, there was sufficient open land at that time and no real cause for alarm arose at the loss of common or amenity.

Under the terms of his father's will, Sir Thomas was able to let out the two non-Heath estates on leases of only 21 years. Obviously such a short span would attract agriculture rather than building.

The construction of Finchley Road changed the time-honoured situation as far as Sir Thomas was concerned, because his fields on either side of the road were eligible, if not ripe, for building development. He could break the terms of his father's will by two methods: he could obtain a private Act of Parliament to do so or, if he had a son and heir who had reached the age of 21, they could jointly agree to vary the settlement terms. Sir Thomas, however, was unmarried and remained so. Therefore he promoted a perfectly straightforward Act of Parliament in 1829, similar to many obtained by other landowners, seeking powers to vary the will so as to grant 99-year building leases on his Hampstead estate. This would probably have been passed without much notice, since the Hampstead fields were neither here nor there in the ample acres around London, but he tacked on, as if by afterthought, an application to build on the Heath as well. This infuriated some copyholders, who petitioned against the Bill.

The Heath was already held in some regard outside the locality. This is made plain in the words of Sir Charles Burrell, a Sussex landowner who, in supporting Sir Thomas, said 'that the Lord of the Manor of Hampstead ought

*54. Sir Thomas Maryon Wilson.*

not to be precluded from improving his property with the consent of the copyholders, because the tradesmen of the Metropolis chose to make it a place of recreation for themselves, their wives, children and friends.' The reaction of the Press was hostile to the Bill and it was lost in the Commons. Sir Thomas returned, duly chastened, in 1830 with a Bill which excluded the Heath, but the damage was done – he was now too late to escape opposition, however unfair. The residents now argued that if he was allowed to build on the East Park estate then the East Heath would be surrounded on three sides by houses and its charm lost. In this they were right, but such scenic niceties had no basis in law, and it was the terms of the will which won the day. Sir Thomas was driven back again.

The matter was now a *cause célèbre*, famous enough to be recalled when, in 1843, after a period of building recession, Sir Thomas renewed his efforts. If, at this stage, he had dropped not only the Heath but the East Park estate as well, he would probably have got through a Bill which placed at his disposal more than enough land near the Finchley Road to build on – enough, at any rate, to stretch his resources for a very long time. But Sir Thomas was an obstinate man who was not prepared to accept that sort of compromise. As far as he was concerned the East Park fields were his and should be available for exploitation along with the rest. As a last resort he could, legally, have built on the estates himself using his own money, but he was either too proud, too cautious or too poor to attempt it then. Once again his Bill was thrown out, and each defeat made the cause more famous.

*55. John Gurney
Hoare, by
G. Richmond, 1855.*

The following year he tried a different tack. If he could obtain permission from Parliament to sell his estate – even that was prohibited by the will – he could obtain something like a building price for the land and the purchasers would have an automatic right to develop it. Again the residents opposed this clear deviation from the will. However inconvenient to the son, Parliament again declined.

Eventually Sir Thomas conceded, in as much as he began building on the East Park estate himself, using his own money. He planned an ornamental park containing 28 villas; he built a rudimentary road, a wall and gatekeeper's hut, all of which survive, and then, in 1845, commenced on the vital viaduct. Fortunately for later generations the viaduct was handsome and expensive to build because of landslips and water penetration, and it gave Sir Thomas a salutary lesson in the pitfalls of building. He retired hurt once more.

In the 1850s, when Sir Thomas presented a fifth Bill, the residents were led not by unsophisticated copyholders but by articulate professionals such as banker John Gurney Hoare, who lived at The Hill. Supporting him were the most influential residents of the town, including the Vestry, organised and willing to continue the fight. Their obduracy was tested in 1854. Sir Thomas, at last, presented a Bill which excluded the Heath and the East Park. The dilemma for the residents was that although they had no objection to building on the Finchley Road estate they feared that if permission to vary the will was granted once, it could be granted twice at the expense of the East Park estate. This is one interpretation of the opposition's motives at the time, but Professor Thompson is more suspicious. Could it be that the leaders of the campaign, living in houses which boasted the unspoilt Heath as their main

73

asset, had self-serving motives disguised as a campaign for the common good? The residents, at any rate, offered Sir Thomas a compromise: they would not oppose the Bill if he *publicly* pledged not to try to build on East Park. He turned them down and the battle moved to the next stage.

At this point a change in the procedure of the law was before Parliament. A new Bill allowed applications to vary the terms of a will to be heard by a Chancery judge instead of before the full gaze of Parliament. The residents feared that without their allies in Parliament the cause could be lost, and they therefore contrived to have inserted into the new Bill a clause to exclude any person who had previously applied for a variance and had been refused. Everyone knew that the only person to be affected by this clause would be Sir Thomas, a singling-out which struck some people as not quite British, and it was only with some difficulty that the Bill, with this clause included, was passed.

While Sir Thomas made several fruitless attempts to remove the 'exclusion' clause, the residents tried to influence the government as to the desirability of buying the Heath. The Commons Preservation Society, formed in 1865, for the urgent task of saving commons all over the country, took the lead on Hampstead Heath, quite the most important example. Sir Thomas was making difficulties all the time; he threatened again to build on the Heath, he allowed it to be excessively excavated for sand and gravel, and the East Park estate was disfigured by a brickfield. When approached by the Metropolitan Board of Works to discuss the public acquisition of the Heath he asked a figure well beyond any possibility.

In 1867 a court case began which was both a culmination and an anti-climax to the battle. It was thought that some judgement would be made which defined the rights of lord and copyholder in the matter of common land, and therefore the consequences would be far-reaching. The Master of the Rolls, however, declined to gamble his reputation and gave no such ruling, and the Commons Preservation Society, faced with prolonged litigation, was entitled to heave a sigh of relief when Sir Thomas died in 1869.

The purchase of the Heath from Sir Thomas's brother and heir, Sir John, by the Metropolitan Board of Works, was made at a brisk pace and by 1872 the Heath was formally declared a public property. No doubt Sir John knew that purchase was inevitable, but he got a good price for it. More to the point now were the East Park estate and Parliament Hill Fields. The former, of course, still belonged to Sir John, but the Fields were part of the lands of the 4th Earl of Mansfield of Kenwood. The East Park estate was difficult to exploit due to access and drainage problems, let alone the furore which might be renewed; in any case, the Maryon Wilson family was occupied enough on the Finchley Road estate. For his part the Earl of Mansfield showed no sign of wanting to spoil his view with houses on the Fields, and so there was a breathing space. It was not until 1884, that a Liberal MP, Sir George Shaw-Lefevre, promoted a meeting at the Assembly Rooms to gauge public response to a new campaign to buy the two properties. It was obvious that only a building-land price would suffice this time, since both pieces of land were free of the encumbrances which had inhibited Sir Thomas.

The MBW was pressed to acquire the properties but declined. Philanthro-

56. *Thomas J. Barratt.*
*Photograph publ. in*
*his* Annals of
Hampstead *(1912).*

pists such as Baroness Burdett-Coutts and Octavia Hill joined the fight, St
Pancras and Hampstead vestries pledged considerable sums, as did the City
of London Parochial Charities fund, and the MBW was asked to find the rest.
This latter body, however, consisted of members from each of the parishes,
and those who came from areas far from Hampstead were not at all impressed
by a plea to make their own constituents pay for more open space for an area
already so well endowed. Finally the MBW offered a sum which made a large
public appeal necessary: £50,000 was needed, and it was found. In 1889 East
Park and Parliament Hill were added to the Heath.

*Hampstead 1000*

Much of the rest of the Heath is outside the Hampstead borders, but needs mention.

The Golders Hill estate was established in the 1760s by Charles Dingley, a wealthy businessman and sycophantic politician.[1] The last owner of the mansion, which was demolished due to war damage, was Sir Spencer Wells; after his death it was auctioned in 1897 together with the grounds, but failed to reach the reserve price and was withdrawn. A second auction was arranged in 1898; this time a number of residents combined to guarantee their own money up to a bid of £35,000. Private bidders sent the price above their limit, but fortunately Thomas Barratt, Chairman of Pears Soap and later author of *The Annals of Hampstead*, who lived at Bellmoor, carried on bidding on his own account and bought the estate for £38,000. Such virtue was repaid when a public appeal raised the whole sum to be paid back to the guarantors, and Golders Hill Park was opened in 1898.

A nail-biting sequence also occurred in the saving of Kenwood House. Kenwood and its grounds were first put up for sale in 1914. The estate consisted of the famous house, two woods, two lakes, farmland and three of the Highgate ponds. Fund-raising, this time led by Sir Arthur Crosfield, who built Witanhurst in Highgate, brought in only enough to buy the meadows

*57. Gipsies encamped on Fortune Green. Photograph by W. D. Cochrane c.1887.*

76

58. *Samuel and Henrietta Barnett.*

south of the two woods in 1922. Three years later the south wood and the two lakes were added, but the house and its adjacent grounds were a tougher hurdle. Neither government nor the London County Council would help in this vital purchase, and defeat seemed certain until the 1st Earl of Iveagh, a member of the Guinness family, bought the house for £107,000, refurbished it and guaranteed it to the nation on his death. It was opened to the public in 1928.

What is now called the Heath Extension was part of the old Wyldes Farm estate. In 1889 Henrietta Barnett and her husband Samuel, a clergyman in London's east end, took Heath End House near the Spaniards for a weekend retreat. Some years later the Charing Cross, Euston and Hampstead Railway, forerunner of the Northern line, announced that *en route* to its projected terminus at Golders Green there would be a station at North End near Wyldes Farm. This, in turn, would have brought development to the Wyldes Estate, still owned by Eton College. Henrietta Barnett organised a Heath Extension Council which obtained an option to buy. Optimistic hopes of high donations from the LCC and the London boroughs were dashed, and with a shortfall of £5000 it was Thomas Barratt, again, who was instrumental with friends, in guaranteeing the rest of the money needed. The land was bought in 1904, leaving the space open and the railway station unnecessary. At the same time Henrietta Barnett bought the rest of Wyldes Estate and on this founded the Hampstead Garden Suburb.[2]

Other open spaces in Hampstead were ornamental compared with these ample acres, but they were no less keenly fought for. West End Green, for example, was the scene of direct action by local residents, and its preservation was a victory for them and without credit to the Vestry. In 1875 John Culverhouse, with a lease on the Green from the lord of the manor, put hoardings round it prior to beginning development. These were torn down by the local people. After a period of simmering the Green was put up for sale at £850, which the Vestry agreed to pay provided that the MBW put up half the money. The Vestry rescinded its decision the following year and offered only £500, laying itself open to the accusation that while it was prepared to spend thousands on improvements at the top of Fitzjohn's Avenue it was not able to afford a few hundred on West End. The vendor therefore sold the Green privately for £850 to a Mr Fowle, who put up hoardings of a more substantial nature. On a wet Monday night in July 1882 some two hundred men converged on the Green armed with axes, crowbars and a large can of oil. They outnumbered the solitary policeman on guard, tore down the hoardings and set fire to them. In the end the Vestry did not increase its offer and the local residents had to find the extra £350.

The Vestry was not much more active in the matter of Fortune Green. In 1888 the Kent, Sussex and General Land Company offered the owner, again Mr Culverhouse, £1200 for the Green, with a view to building on it. The Company withdrew in face of local opposition but residents were sufficiently alarmed about public access by then to evict with zeal some gipsies who pitched there in 1893. The question of ownership went to court, where the Vestry, pleading that the Green had always been used for public recreation, produced witnesses who had played cricket, quoits and trapball in the 1830s; the heirs to the late Mr Culverhouse contended that although the odd casual game might be played the Green was principally used by laundresses, from whom they obtained a regular rent. The judge, while sympathising with the Vestry, found for the Culverhouse party. Another fund-raising campaign was mounted and with grants from a reluctant Vestry, the LCC and local residents, the Green was laid out in 1898.

[1] See p. 53.
[2] The best accounts of the battles for these open spaces are contained in: Alan Farmer, *Hampstead Heath* (1984), Christopher Ikin, *Hampstead Heath Centenary* (1971, repr. 1985) and Professor F. M. L. Thompson op. cit.

# CHAPTER SEVEN
# Estates Divided

The development of the fields of Hampstead was related to the campaign to save the Heath. The long dispute between the lord of the manor and various residents froze the Maryon Wilson estate, much the largest in Hampstead, and thus allowed builders the opportunity to develop, with some panache, less promising areas. If buildings of the quality of those on the Eton and Belsize estates had been erected in the 1840s and 1850s on Maryon Wilson land they would have absorbed, having the better locations, whatever custom there was for distinctive houses. Hampstead's architectural pattern, most likely, would have been inverted so that Belsize became the Edwardian area.

Few of the new roads were built with railway access in mind – unusual for London – and this bears witness to Hampstead having scenic and social merits which were attractive enough in their own rights to invite new residents. Only one estate, St John's Park, east of Haverstock Hill, could be said to have been erected with a shrewd eye to the early march of sleepers.

The first serious development began in 1830 at today's triangle of roads of which Chalk Farm Underground station is the apex. Adelaide Road and the railway to Euston did not exist and the houses built in this area were secluded villas in abundant grounds which lent themselves readily to maximum profit in the 1930s when they were replaced by mansion flats. The impetus for this, albeit limited, building spate was an optimistic view that the prestigious development of Regent's Park would have a beneficial effect on the Eton College estate. Primrose Hill, which was part of the Eton College land, was nearer to Regent's Park but it was not adjacent to a main road at the time and access would have been prohibitive. Building began, instead, on a part of the Eton estate nearest to a turnpike road (Haverstock Hill); Primrose Hill, to the delight of future walkers, was traded with the Crown twelve years later for land in Eton.

Building was slow, however. Adelaide Road did not reach Swiss Cottage until about 1850. There it met not only the Finchley Road but the new roads just built on the Eyre estate, such as Avenue Road and St John's Wood Park. As development slowly consumed both sides of Adelaide Road, the Swiss Cottage area, previously a meeting-place of cart-tracks, became an important hub for traffic. The area received its name from the tavern which, built in the Swiss style in vogue at the time, opened in about 1840. It was joined in 1851 by the theological New College in College Crescent and between it and its chapel on the site of Swiss Cottage library there was a school for the blind and a large mansion called Sunnyside.

If Eton College was leisurely in exploiting its lands then the Dean and Chapter of Westminster, the ground landlords of the Belsize estate, were positively tardy. In 1807 their lessee, the Earl of Chesterfield, sold his interest to four Hampstead men, James Abel, Thomas Forsyth, Germain Lavie and Thomas Roberts, who divided the estate into eight portions, each of which had a separate lease. The tenure of each lease was dependent on the life spans of three people whose names were written in to each agreement; when one of the 'lives' died or 'dropped', a new one could be inserted on payment of a fee. This fragmentation was to cause problems later for the Dean and Chapter as the leases fell in at different and unpredictable times.

These small estates became 'parks' – the fashionable word for the time – and in most a sizeable villa, secluded from the main road, was built in a good imitation of a rural retreat. Otherwise an original house was kept. Belsize House was still there, at that time occupied by Spencer Perceval, later to be the only British prime minister to be assassinated; the 18th-century Rosslyn House, further north, had been the home of the Earl of Rosslyn, Lord Chancellor from 1793, who was generally thought to be savagely excessive in his treatment of those accused of promoting social upheaval at the end of the 18th century.

The first park to be developed was on the other side of the road, inexplicably called St John's Park. William Lund, who lived in Haverstock Lodge on the site of Downside Crescent, began building Lawn Road, Upper Park Road and Parkhill Road soon after the clumsily-named East and West India Dock and Birmingham Junction Railway opened its station, now called Primrose Hill, in 1851. Sheltered from these roads, his Lodge remained until the 1890s. The quality of the estate deteriorated as it neared what became Fleet Road in the later 1860s. Not only was the river Fleet an open sewer but in 1869 the smallpox hospital began nearby, an event from which William Lund's estate never recovered.

Belsize Park, which contained Belsize House, was begun in 1853 by Charles Palmer. His intention was to develop an exclusive estate with its own square and church, the access roads of which would deter through traffic. Significantly, the building began at Buckland Crescent near to Swiss Cottage, which underlined the shift of Hampstead westwards even if social influence remained with the old town. Palmer's plan, to isolate the estate from others, was not practical and roads were opened not only from Haverstock Hill to Swiss Cottage but into Englands Lane as well.

Professor Thompson points out[1] that the social class catered for at Belsize was higher than that which lived on the Eton College estate. It preferred, however, to rely on public omnibuses or hired carriage instead of keeping personal conveyances. Consequently there was little provision at first for stabling on the estate and almost an absence of mews properties; provision was mainly incorporated in the odd pocket of land around what is today's Belsize Village.

Rosslyn Park began at the same time, 1853. The lease was held by a City merchant, Henry Davidson. In the 1850s there was a good possibility that Sir Thomas Maryon Wilson might win one of his estate Bills and begin development west of the High Street, and so Davidson decided to pre-empt him; no

59. Rosslyn House by
J. P. Emslie, 1896.

60. The Rookery,
Greenhill. The
residence of Thomas
Norton Longman,
from a drawing by
R.B.S. (probably
R. B. Schnebellie).

81

sooner had he embarked on his plan for Thurlow and Lyndhurst Roads than a scheme was announced to build the Hampstead Junction Railway beneath his land. This seriously delayed the building activities.

By the 1880s most of the Dean and Chapter's estate was built upon except where old mansions and their grounds survived. Ivy Bank, for example, the house where Sir Arnold Bax was born, was not replaced by Perceval Avenue until 1914.

North of the Westminster land was the Greenhill estate which stretched from just below the King William IV to Thurlow Road. This was laid out in the 1870s. On it existed the distinguished group of houses (Nos. 85–8) in the High Street which included Stanfield House, a large mansion called The Rookery occupied by the Longman family, and the old Vane House which had been partly rebuilt and occupied by the Royal Soldiers' Daughters Home, an institution founded soon after the end of the Crimean war. Longman's house had gone by 1872, to be replaced by a Wesleyan chapel which itself was displaced in the 1930s by the Greenhill flats; a remnant of Vane House survived until 1970. Ellerdale Road and the top end of Arkwright Road, seemingly part of the Maryon Wilson development, were in fact part of the Greenhill estate and were laid out, if not built, in 1871. This was after Hampstead had recovered from the considerable shock of Parliament agreeing to an extension of the Metropolitan and St John's Wood railway, which had reached Swiss Cottage by 1868. It was proposed that the line should proceed on the surface across Maryon Wilson fields, go through a

*61. The Logs, Nos. 17–20 East Heath Road. Built by J. S. Nightingale in 1868.*

tunnel when it reached Greenhill, cross the High Street on a bridge by the King William IV, and have a terminus at Willow Road. It has to be said that Hampstead Vestry did not oppose this plan, other than to make sure its sewers were safeguarded, which reveals a disregard for the character and peace of the town that is almost breathtaking. This ill-judged scheme founded not on opposition, but through lack of funds.[2]

By 1871 the Heath was safe from builders, Sir Thomas Maryon Wilson was dead with scarce a tear shed, and the legal position more conducive to development of his estate. The battle for the East Park estate was still to come and it was fortunate for the later campaigners that this beautiful stretch of land was so inaccessible. This situation was exacerbated in 1871 when Thomas Rhodes, a large landowner in north London, began to build South Hill Park, an odd loop of road which effectively blocked off the East Park estate from South End Green. It was an unfriendly development by Rhodes, and meant to be, but at least it created what most people think is an unusual and charming view of the backs of houses across Hampstead ponds.

After all the fuss made by the Maryon Wilsons to have the facility to develop their lands, they were slow off the mark once they were able to. Partly, as Professor Thompson points out, this was due to differences of opinion between Sir John and his son Spencer, who needed to act in unison to break the restrictions of the will.

Priory Road was begun first, in 1874. At the western edge of the estate, it would provide access to that congested area of houses containing Broadhurst,

*62. 'Beauchêne' in Fitzjohn's Avenue.*

83

Compayne, Canfield, Greencroft and Aberdare Gardens, and Goldhurst Terrace. The following year the line of Fitzjohn's Avenue, the showpiece of the estate, was laid out. It should be remembered that this could go only as far as Arkwright Road – there was no extension, then, to Heath Street. Between Perrins Lane and Holly Hill was a jumble of courtyards and alleys, the oldest part of town, which was quite unsuitable for carriage traffic. The Vestry was asked to apply to the MBW to sweep away this picturesque squalor so that Fitzjohn's Avenue could reach the centre of town, but there was opposition from traders who had strong influence on the Vestry, as they envisaged traffic going through Hampstead without touching the High Street. One suggestion was that the traffic should be routed down the newly-formed Prince Arthur Road into the High Street. The difficulty here was that the top of the High Street was considerably narrower than it is today – it was little more than the width of Holly Hill – and had been for years the cause of congestion and complaints.

There was no choice eventually. The whole, triangular, area was razed, the High Street widened while they were at it, model dwellings built by the Wells and Campden charity, and the Fitzjohn's Avenue extension built, though the antagonism between the Vestry and the Maryon Wilsons is, perhaps, reflected in the fact that this was illogically numbered as part of Heath Street and not the Avenue.

One of the results of these town improvements, easily distinguished in the large-scale red-brick building in the area, was that the new shops could accommodate such multiples as Woolworth's, Express Dairies and Sains-

*Opposite:*
*63. The rear view of the Chicken House, Hampstead High Street, 1879.*

*64. The old Workhouse, Frognal, c.1805.*

bury's, until the economics of modern retailing forced them out again.

The size and architectural style of the houses in Fitzjohn's Avenue make it unique in London. The 'boulevard' effect was novel and popular, and in London terms, wasteful of space, but Spencer Wilson, whose project it was,[3] gambled correctly and attracted the right leaseholders. Vast houses were built, many of which survive, such as No. 55, which had 25 rooms, panelled drawing-rooms and a hand-painted Monk organ on the first landing.

In the 1840s, the hamlet of West End consisted of a number of large houses, at least two inns, a village green with a pond, and very little else.[4] Even in 1864, with two railways cut across its southern end, this rural scene had hardly changed. Fields or gardens stretched in all directions, particularly down to the scarcely inhabited main road to Edgware.

North of West End there were three substantial houses built in the first half of the 19th century. Thomas Pell Platt, an oriental scholar whose credentials rested on a translation of the Bible into Ethiopian,[5] built Childs Hill House on the site of the present Rosecroft Avenue area; he died in 1852 and his house was pulled down in 1903. John Teil, an East India merchant with tanneries in Kidderpore, Calcutta,[6] built Kidderpore Hall in 1843; this was transformed into a neo-Grecian building by Charles Cannon, the warranted dyer to Queen Victoria. He died in 1876 and his estate, too early on the market to attract development, was partly used by the West Middlesex Water Company for a reservoir. The house was taken by Westfield College in 1890 when the rest of his estate was built on. Henry Weech Burgess built Burgess Park and his son began development in the 1860s, the mansion becoming the Anglo-French College.

Given that from the 1870s new buildings pressed in from several directions, and that railways ran through the southern end, it is surprising that most of the mansions of West End lasted until the 1890s. An early casualty was West

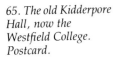

*65. The old Kidderpore Hall, now the Westfield College. Postcard.*

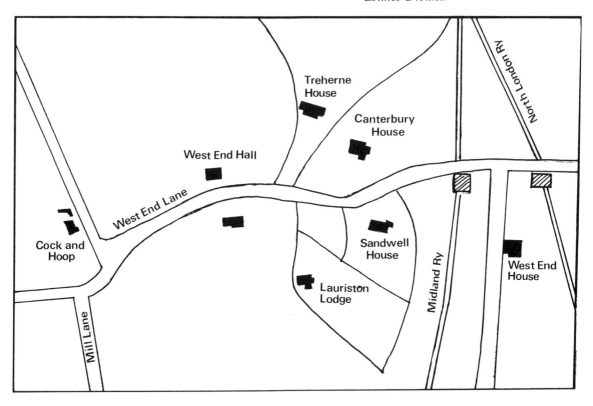

66. Plan of the
principal houses of
West End, mid-19th
century.

67. William Beckford.

*Holl sculp.*

*68. Jack Straw's Castle tea gardens, c.1835. From a watercolour.*

*Opposite:*
*69. The Firs, near the Spaniards. From a watercolour.*

End House in the south. The Hampstead Junction Railway cut past its back door in 1860, and eight years later the Midland Railway crossed its front, leaving the house isolated and facing inevitable demolition. This house, or an earlier form of it, was the home, in 1762, of William Beckford who was twice Lord Mayor of London. Shortly before his death in 1770 he achieved notoriety for publicly remonstrating with George III after the king had refused to consider a petition relating to a recent election. This unheard-of effrontery earned him popular regard and led to all of the 244 words of his speech being engraved on the pillar of his statue at the Guildhall. Beckford, who was able to exploit slaves on his Jamaica estate, died immensely rich – he left £1 million and an annual income of £100,000.

Railways effectively killed whatever chance there might have been of low-density housing to the west of West End Lane. Slivers and triangles of land were created by the lines, some taken by marshalling yards, some by brickfields, some by warehousing. It was not surprising that the streets squeezed into the remaining areas, mostly run up by property companies for first-time buyers with moderate incomes, should quickly become lodging houses once the noise and dirt of the railways had been suffered; the new underground railway hastened this change to commuter-land.

To the north the Shoot-up Hill estate was held, at this time, by Colonel Percy Cotton, whose travels abroad were the inspiration for his choice of such

*70. Platts Lane.*
*Postcard.*

street names as Rondu and Skardu Roads. He lived at a house called Kings-gate which was an enlarged version of the old Shoot-up Hill farm – Kingscroft Road, built in 1912–13, is now on the site. Cotton held not only this estate but the remnants of the old Kilburn Priory land either side of West End Lane, and he peppered both properties with street names reflecting his estate on the Isle of Thanet as well as his colonial glories. Development of Shoot-up Hill was blighted by the railway and by the siting of the new cemetery at Fortune Green.

Another mansion to survive until quite late was Oak Lodge, later to be called The Grange, off Kilburn High Road. The last owner was a Mrs Peters, a coachbuilder's widow, who established a literary salon here. The house and grounds, together with five acres of market-garden, were bought by Hampstead Borough Council in 1912 for £5500, for use as a public park.[7]

The southernmost part of the Kilburn estate was begun and abruptly halted, as we have seen,[8] c.1810. This land was inherited in 1845 by Colonel Arthur Upton who continued Greville Road and also built Mortimer Road and Kilburn Priory to a good standard, but the neighbourhood was not prestigious enough to merit the same style.

Three further areas need to be mentioned. The first is Oak Hill Park in Frognal. This was built on a small close in 1856 by Sir Thomas Neave of nearby Branch Hill Lodge. He also possessed a collection of stained glass which included the window from the Chicken House, Rosslyn Hill, depicting the 17th-century visit of James I.

The second is the Carlile House estate, off Rosslyn Hill. Its exploitation was delayed until 1876, when a property company took over and packed in the middle-class houses of Kemplay, Willoughby and Carlingford Roads, and Rudall Crescent.

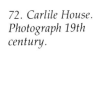

71. *Finchley Road. Postcard.*

72. *Carlile House. Photograph 19th century.*

The third was the South End Green area. Thomas Rhodes had already built South Hill Park and Gardens to a standard which augured well for the nearby Pickett's Farm, now cut in half by the railway. Pickett turned developer on a shoestring, and finished Parliament Hill and Nassington Road. Both of these roads, as Professor Thompson points out,[9] finish abruptly at Parliament Hill Fields over which, it was expected, they would be extended in the not too distant future. Pickett also waged a campaign to remove the unsavoury pond by South End Road; in this he was successful in 1885, the year he finished Tanza Road. The nearby picturesque hexagonal water tower, on the site of a well sunk by the Hampstead Water Company in 1835, lasted until 1907.

It seemed, at this period, as though South End Green was set for a medium-to-good development. Mrs Crump, of Hereford House (on the site of the Classic cinema), presented a drinking fountain in 1881 'for 16 persons at one time and four troughs for dogs', but the advent of the smallpox hospital and the uncertainty about its future blighted the half of Pickett's Farm on the other side of the railway line, now the site of Agincourt, Constantine and Cressy Roads. It had been owned by St Pancras vestryman and estate agent Joseph Salter; he died, leaving twelve children and their care and financial interests in the hands of Thomas Eccleston Gibb, the former Vestry Clerk of St Pancras, who also bought into the estate. There was no chance at all of this area being of any distinction. The hospital made it undesirable, as did the polluted Fleet;

*Opposite:*
*73. Frognal Priory c.1859.*

*74. Erskine House by J. Appleton, 1890.*

*75. Heath Mount School by G. S. Shepperd, 1830.*

then the London Street Tramways obtained an extension up Fleet Road to the terminus at South End Green, thereby settling the social tone. Finally, despite its geographical position as part of Hampstead, it was identified in the public eye with the artisans' houses of Gospel Oak.

When the last roads of this much blighted estate were finished in the late 1890s, Hampstead's building spree was almost over.

[1] Professor F. M. L. Thompson, op. cit., p. 278.
[2] See Michael Alpert's article on West Hampstead railways in *Camden History Review* No. 7. He contends that the plan was lost mainly because of public opposition.
[3] Professor F. M. L. Thompson, op. cit., p. 312.
[4] See illustration 66.
[5] Christopher Wade, *The Streets of Hampstead*, p. 22 (rev. 1984).
[6] Anon., *Westfield College 1882–1932*, p. 4 (1932).
[7] Christopher Wade, ed., *The Streets of West Hampstead*, p. 37 (1975). This book contains a great deal of information about the development of this side of Hampstead, on which I have drawn frequently. So, too, does Professor F. M. L. Thompson's, op. cit.
[8] See p. 52.
[9] Professor F. M. L. Thompson, op. cit., p. 353.

# CHAPTER EIGHT

# Traversed by Lines

With few exceptions transport in Hampstead has followed the population; generally it did not, as in many parts of outer London, inspire or hasten development, although in some areas of Hampstead it had the effect of lowering the quality of the housing which came later.

Before the advent of the horse omnibus in the mid-1830s the limited needs of Hampstead residents to get to the City or the west end of London, were met by short-stage coaches. The principal boarding point in Hampstead was by the old Bird-in-Hand public house at the top of the High Street, and the horses were changed, rested or fed in Norway Yard – later the Blue Star garage site which, of course, was the scene of similar services for the horses' mechanical successor. By 1825 there were 10 coaches serving Hampstead.[1]

The two-decker horse omnibus could take 26 passengers. Undoubtedly the hills of Hampstead were cruel on the horses, especially as the buses not only stopped at fixed stages but could be hailed at any point on their journey – an interruption of momentum particularly hard on the animals. The routes were usually identified by the colour of the coaches – that from Hampstead to St Giles-in-the-Fields, for example, had yellow vehicles.

The horse's life was made marginally easier with the introduction of the horse tram which itself was a development from the 18th-century horse railways used in industrial areas. The tramways began in earnest in the 1870s but Hampstead residents would have none of them in the parish fearing not only the noise, but the lowering of the social tone of the village.[2]

The residents also successfully opposed a proposal in 1883 to build a tramway on which the cars were hauled up Hampstead High Street by cable – a similar scheme was already being constructed up Highgate Hill from the Archway Tavern and was to open the following year.[3]

The only tram line to penetrate the parish borders was that of the London Street Tramways who constructed a spur to their Gospel Oak line, which ran from Southampton Road, along Fleet Road and terminated at South End Green. This was to provide transport for many people to the Heath but it also made certain the essentially poor-class housing development of this area. In 1901 the London County Council built a one-way extension of this line back down Agincourt Road to Southampton Road, which not only facilitated traffic but helped entrance and exit at the large depot and works which had been constructed at Cressy Road. This portion of line was the last in London to be specifically built for horse trams.[4] Electrification of tramways began all over London within ten years and it consigned many horses and their managers and providers to an unexpected redundancy.

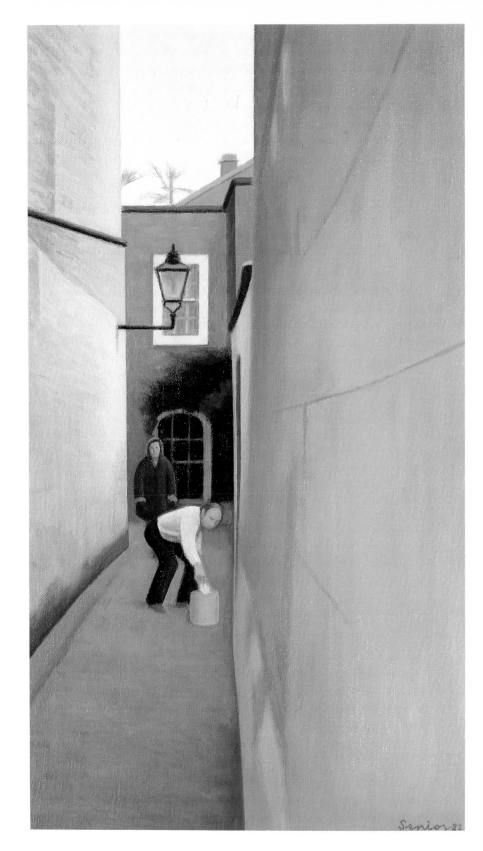

*76. Painting a wall,
Streatley Place, 1982.
Oil on canvas, size
28" × 16", by Bryan
Senior, born 1935.*

77. *Horse bus in West End Lane. Postcard.*

78. *Transport in Finchley Road. Postcard.*

A horse bus route went up the Finchley Road to the Metropolitan line station of that name which was opened in 1879, but extension of the bus route was unnecessary as there was not enough development either side of Finchley Road to make it worthwhile. By the end of the 19th century horse buses went as far as Cricklewood Lane from both Finchley Road and West End Lane.[5]

97

79. Kilburn to London
motor bus. Postcard.

The first railway through Hampstead, in 1837, had no station within the parish boundaries, although there was one just outside near the Roundhouse at Chalk Farm. The London to Birmingham Railway, later the London and North Western ran through Eton College land in the much-admired Primrose Hill tunnel. So rural was Hampstead then that except by the Kilburn High Road it is doubtful if a single house was displaced on its route through the southern edge of the parish.

In 1851 the East and West India Docks and Birmingham Junction Railway (later called the North London Railway) was connected to the LNWR near the Roundhouse, and by 1852 freight could be diverted off the main LNWR line right down to the docks in the east end of London. The promoters of this railway, which did so much to hasten the decline of some areas of Camden and Kentish Towns by its construction of roof-level viaducts, were surprised to find that it was much in demand by passengers because it provided access to the City. Boosted by this unexpected custom the promoters built an expensive spur from Dalston down to their prestigious new terminus at Broad Street in 1865.

On its approach to Camden Town the LNWR line had become very congested. The Company baulked at the expense of doubling the size of its track through the Primrose Hill tunnel, although it had to later, and promoted instead the Hampstead Junction Railway which was a large loop going through the almost open countryside via Gospel Oak, Hampstead Heath, Finchley Road and Brondesbury, to connect again with the main LNWR line at Willesden. This bypass, now commonly called the Broad Street–Richmond line, opened in 1860 but it was some years before it had a population along it to make passenger travel profitable. Illustration 80 depicts Finchley Road station in 1860, surrounded by fields. Hampstead Heath station was much in demand, however, especially at weekends and bank holidays, when east-

enders could get to it very easily. On Easter Monday in 1892 the size of the crowd returning to the station after a sudden deluge of rain caused the death of two women and six children who were crushed on the staircase to the platforms.

Two more railways reached Hampstead in 1868. The Midland extended its line from Bedford to St Pancras, sweeping through the Shoot-up Hill area at surface level, and then tunnelling from Finchley Road to Gospel Oak. This considerate approach was abandoned completely as it bulldozed its way through to Somers Town but at least it had the merit of obliterating the notorious Agar Town. The Midland Railway helped to cut up West Hampstead into difficult pieces as well as delaying development in the Lyndhurst Gardens area where it was in a tunnel.

Also, in 1868, the Metropolitan Line reached Swiss Cottage. This line had its origins in the first underground railway in London which opened in 1863 from Farringdon to Baker Street. It was constructed, not by tunnelling, but by a cut-and-cover method beneath the main streets. It was a great success and the following year the promoters opened extensions to the populated areas of Ladbroke Grove and Hammersmith. It then launched on two costly lines, one via Paddington down to Gloucester Road to form, later, one segment of the Circle Line, and another up to the good-class area of St Johns Wood with a terminus at the relatively unpopulated Swiss Cottage. These efforts exhausted the Company's funds and it was not until 1879 that the Metropolitan was extended to Finchley Road, West Hampstead, Kilburn and Willesden, on its journey into John Betjeman's 'Metroland'. In 1939 this route through Hampstead and St Johns Wood was duplicated by the Bakerloo Line (now the Jubilee Line).[6]

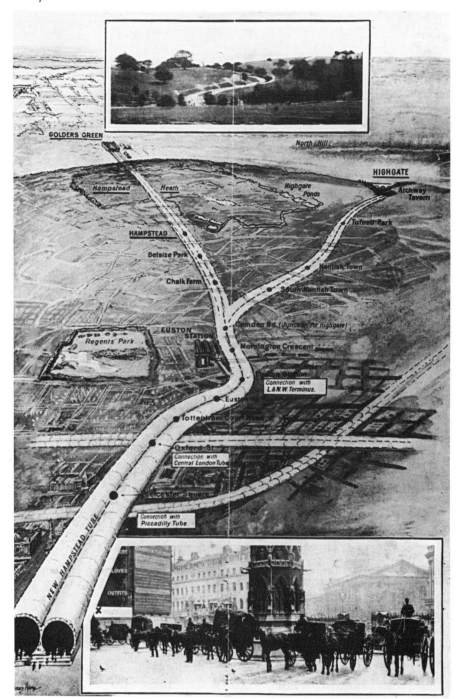

81. 'How the new tube
railway reached
Hampstead from
Charing Cross.'
London Transport
Executive, 1907.

82. Map of railways
across West
Hampstead. By kind
permission of the
compiler, Michael
Alpert, and the
Camden History
Society. From the
Camden History
Review, Vol. 7.

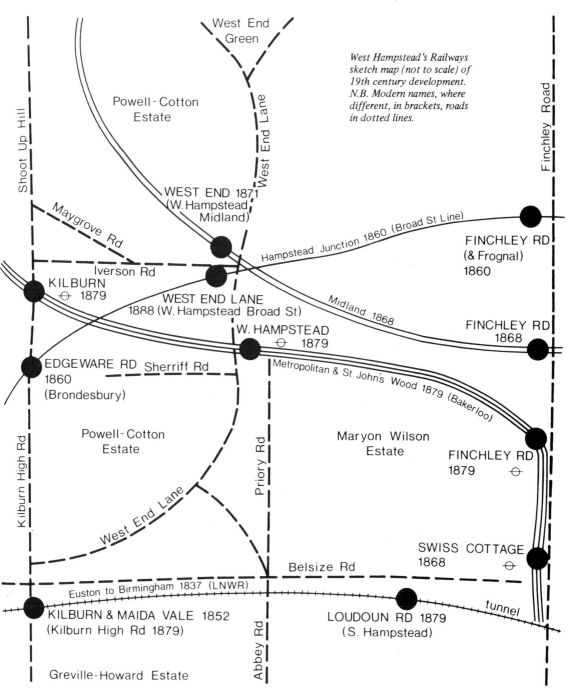

West End
Green

Powell-Cotton
Estate

*West Hampstead's Railways
sketch map (not to scale) of
19th century development.
N.B. Modern names, where
different, in brackets, roads
in dotted lines.*

Shoot Up Hill

Finchley Road

West End Lane

Maygrove Rd

WEST END 1871
(W. Hampstead
Midland)

Hampstead Junction 1860 (Broad St Line)

FINCHLEY RD
(& Frognal)
1860

Iverson Rd

KILBURN
⊖ 1879

WEST END LANE
1888 (W. Hampstead Broad St)

Midland 1868

FINCHLEY RD
1868

W. HAMPSTEAD
⊖ 1879

EDGEWARE RD
1860
(Brondesbury)

Sherriff Rd

Metropolitan & St John's Wood 1879 (Bakerloo)

Powell-Cotton
Estate

Priory Rd

Maryon Wilson
Estate

FINCHLEY RD
1879 ⊖

Kilburn High Rd

West End Lane

SWISS COTTAGE
1868 ⊖

Belsize Rd

Euston to Birmingham 1837 (LNWR)

tunnel

KILBURN & MAIDA VALE 1852
(Kilburn High Rd 1879)

Abbey Rd

LOUDOUN RD 1879
(S. Hampstead)

Greville-Howard Estate

101

South End Road                                           Hampstead

HAMPSTEAD H
LONDON & NORTH WESTERN
TRAINS TO THE CITY KENSINGTON
BIRMINGHAM MANCHESTER LIVER

*83. Hampstead Heath*
*Station. Postcard*
*c.1905.*

The Charing Cross to Hampstead tube was opened by Lloyd George in 1907 and connected to other lines to the south and east to form what is now the Northern Line system. The original powers of the promoters in 1893 were to build a line from the Strand to terminate at Heath Street with a branch to Euston, which was not, then, on the main line.[7] The scheme languished through lack of funds and it was Charles Tyson Yerkes, an enterprising but unscrupulous entrepreneur from Chicago, who rescued it by buying the Company and injecting it with sound finance. During the next few years he was to acquire a number of lines which made up parts of the Underground system, all of which were in various degrees of financial difficulty.

It was Yerkes who proposed the extension of the tube to the open fields of Golders Green with an intermediate station at Jack Straw's Castle. This roused the Hampstead Heath Protection Society against him because it was felt that a tunnel beneath the Heath would act as a drain and therefore damage the surface badly.[8] Hampstead Vestry withdrew its opposition once Yerkes had altered the site of his station to near the Bull and Bush, just outside the parish boundary, and left the Protection Society with a vain fight on its hands. The Bull and Bush platforms were constructed but the station wasn't.[9]

[1] Professor F. M. L. Thompson, op. cit., p. 56
[2] Ibid, p. 364.
[3] John Richardson, op. cit., pp. 197–200.
[4] Charles E. Lee, *Camden History Review*, No. 2, p. 22.
[5] Professor F. M. L. Thompson, op. cit., pp. 58–9.
[6] A full article on railway development in Hampstead, by Michael Alpert, is contained in *Camden History Review*, No. 7.
[7] Charles E. Lee, *Sixty Years of the Northern*, p. 10 (1967).
[8] Alan Farmer, op. cit., p. 134 (1984)
[9] See pp. 77–8.

# CHAPTER NINE
# Artists in their Quarters

It would be tedious to recite the full array of artists, writers, musicians, politicians and other notable people who have lived in Hampstead. A list, by no means comprehensive, is printed in the Appendix. It is unlikely that any other town or borough in Britain, with the exception of Westminster, could claim so many, or have made so much effort to catalogue them in its archives. The steady growth of Hampstead's popularity among students, the professions, artists and the affluent has meant that a disproportionate number of such people, influential in their fields, have at some time lived here.

It is therefore simple in Hampstead to indulge in vicarious thrills, such as treading the walks that sickly John Keats took, or sitting where he sat. Dead artists have this effect on people, while equally gifted lawyers and industrialists, for example, do not. Who goes to Kenwood House and imagines that talented man, the first Lord Mansfield, in its splendour? Who goes to the site of Spedan Tower and thinks of store-owner John Lewis, although, of course, it was his successors who fashioned the nature of his enterprise? Probably very few people. But who stands quietly in the bedroom of Keats House and does not imagine that poet still there in spirit? Or who does not pause to reflect for a moment on encountering the plaque to D. H. Lawrence in the Vale of Health? Very few. And why are so few of the reliable people, bent over their paperwork and their letters to *The Times*, and who helped to save the Heath and its extensions for us, so badly remembered?

There is no logic to this. However short the stay of the artist, however he or she became involved with the life of the town, it is the artist who attracts a romantic and almost uncritical curiosity. Quite often publications gloss over their real lives (except in the case of Lawrence, whose real life was too public) as if it were somehow a betrayal of Hampstead that unpleasantness happened beyond the plaque. We read of the writer Anna Barbauld living a peaceful, literary life in Church Row, with her husband Rochemont, a preacher at the Rosslyn Hill Chapel 'in failing health': the truth is that he was going insane, and their stay in Hampstead must have been distressing for both her and the congregation.

Putting aside such hero-worship, it has to be conceded that the fact or reputation of so many artists in residence has had the effect of drawing to the town those who enjoy the arts and those who wish to be good or outstanding practitioners. The atmosphere of Hampstead is based on the gathering of successful and hopeful, and from this springs the nature of the shops, the

*84. Sir Richard Steele.*
*Publ. 1794.*

pubs, the entertainment and the pronounced street life. Hampstead is still a place where young people, on their own, live in a heady mixture of hope, freedom and seediness. Even the invasion of the affluent, which has ensured that estate agency is the most visible occupation, has not destroyed the essential artiness of the place.

So it would be pedantic in the extreme not to devote a chapter to the notables in any perspective view of Hampstead. As to the Constables, Romneys and Linnells, their story has been related many times and such famous names will be lightly dealt with. Instead, the Hampstead gathering of painters, sculptors, architects, writers, designers and political thinkers in the 1930s, people who helped to change the whole spirit of British art and politics, will be given its due coverage. It is this period which should be the basis for any parochial pride.

Two early famous names were both literary, both used Hampstead as a retreat and both stayed in the same house. Sir Charles Sedley, Restoration wit and writer, had sobered down a rumbustious life by the time he came to Hampstead or, as Barratt put it, 'had come to his better senses'. He was in ill-health and died in a small, white cottage on Haverstock Hill opposite the Load of Hay in 1701. To this same building, in 1712, came Sir Richard Steele, then editor of *The Spectator*, and in retreat from political enemies and creditors, though he remained bold enough during his stay to attend meetings of

85. *George Romney.
From a picture by
himself. Publ. 1817.*

86. *Romney's house in
Holly Bush Hill.*

*87. Joanna Baillie.*

*88. John Keats, drawn by Joseph Severn in January, 1821.*

the Kit-Cat club in the village. This cottage, the subject of innumerable illustrations, survived until 1867. It is now covered by the entrance to Steeles Road.

True 18th-century residents were Henry Flitcroft, architect, and Josiah Boydell, painter and engraver. Flitcroft has already been mentioned in other connections[1] and so has Boydell, who went into business with his uncle, John Boydell, who virtually founded print publishing in this country. In 1786 the uncle overreached himself with the production of a series of 170 prints, taken from paintings specially commissioned from leading artists, illustrating the works of Shakespeare; the paintings were then exhibited in a specially built gallery in Pall Mall. The venture nearly led to his bankruptcy and only the aid of Parliament and the business skill of his nephew saved the business.

One contributor to that gallery was George Romney, fashionable painter of the time who, in 1796, bought the house called The Mount off Heath Street. He was rich enough then to convert the outbuildings and stables at the rear into a studio house which suited him better. This house, in Holly Bush Hill, is now called Romney's House. Unfortunately, his health broke down soon afterwards and he moved out to Kendal, much the worse in pocket. He had spent £2500 on his studio but raised only £400 from its sale.[2]

Romney's neighbour was Joanna Baillie, a writer well-known in her day but now almost entirely a subject for scholars. She stayed 60 years at Bolton House on Windmill Hill, keeping up long friendships, especially with Sir Walter Scott who visited her here, and providing hospitality for the likes of the painter Sir David Wilkie, who borrowed her house for a few months in 1810. Crabb Robinson, who met her here, described her patronisingly: 'She has none of the unpleasant airs too common in literary ladies. Her conversation is sensible.'

The stay of John Keats in Hampstead has often been described and needs

little repetition.[3] He lodged briefly in Well Walk at a postman's house on the site of the Wells Tavern. At this time, 1815–16, a pair of semi-detached villas were being constructed just down the hill by Charles Wentworth Dilke and Charles Armitage Brown, with whom Keats became friends. The two houses were called Wentworth Place. Keats became attached to Fanny Brawne, who sometimes stayed in one of the houses, and when Keats moved into Brown's house the relationship became an engagement. He wrote some of his best work here, including *Ode to a Nightingale*. He left Wentworth Place in 1820 for Italy, where he died.

*89. Leigh Hunt by W. F. Williams.*

*90. John Constable when aged 20.*

One of Keats's friends at this period was Leigh Hunt, the poet, who lived for two brief spells in the Vale of Health. The first came after he had been released from prison for libelling the Prince Regent, although it should be said that in the prison of the day he was allowed two decorated rooms, furniture, including a piano, and the company of his wife and six children. This large family, plus a servant, moved in October 1815 to what is usually described as 'a cottage' in the Vale, where Hunt had a busy social life. They stayed until 1818, but returned for a year or so in 1820. It is still not established which house or houses he occupied.[4]

Painters John Linnell and John Constable were in Hampstead at the same time, though not always on the best of terms. Constable came for summer holidays from 1819, but his principal residence was No. 40 Well Walk, where he lived from 1827 to 1837 and where his wife died in 1828, leaving him with the care of their seven children. Constable's Hampstead paintings are well-known (although they are sometimes topographically imaginative) and give the feel of the Heath before it became more verdant and cultivated.

Linnell first rented the old Wyldes farmhouse in August 1823 for the summer. Constable visited him here, as did William Collins, the painter, who was at the root of several disagreements between Linnell and Constable. Another visitor was the young son of Collins, Wilkie. Linnell also took under his wing at Wyldes the 61-year-old William Blake, now failing in health, reputation and confidence, and introduced him to the young Samuel Palmer who eventually became Linnell's son-in-law.

In the 1830s and 1840s Hampstead's most notable names represented different kinds of creativity. Robert Stephenson, the railway engineer, lived in a house on the site of No. 145 Haverstock Hill from 1835 until 1843. From here he supervised the construction of the sightseeing attraction of that age – the Primrose Hill tunnel, as the London to Birmingham railway approached its Euston terminus. Stephenson was popular with both the people and the establishment, whose pockets he lined if they had been shrewd enough to invest in railway shares, but Hampstead resident Rowland Hill, whose work inspired the introduction of the Penny Post, was the hero of the people only. Successive governments ignored or insulted him. He had remarkable inventiveness and administrative abilities, but no social clout, being merely the son of a lower-middle-class family, and he was offered positions within the Post Office at derisory salaries to help carry out his own scheme at a rank subordinate to officials who loathed him and it. It was left to the public to deal handsomely with him, and a subscription raised £13,000; he was able to take a house in Pond Street and soon to transfer to a mansion called Bartrams on Hampstead Green. He died here in 1879, by then loaded with honours and rewards which even the government could scarcely withhold.

Next door to Hill was Sir Francis Palgrave, historian, whose most important contribution to scholarship was to reorganise the Public Record Office and to begin the long series of printed calendars. Palgrave died at Hampstead in 1861. Also living in the group of houses here was Lord Sidney Godolphin Osborne, a radical whose attacks on the social and political systems of the day had made him notorious. He urged reform in education, women's rights, free trade, sanitation, Irish affairs and, most particularly, the lot of the agricultural labourer.

In 1869 St Stephen's church was built on part of Hampstead Green. Its architect was Samuel Sanders Teulon, who lived in Palgrave's old house, but Hampstead's most famous resident architect was Sir George Gilbert Scott the elder, who was at Admiral's House from 1856 to 1864: he was not the last architect to live in a house entirely different from his own building style. His son, also George Gilbert, lived at No. 26 Church Row, next door to George du Maurier, the author of *Trilby*. The du Maurier family were in Hampstead a long time. Sir Gerald, the actor, was born in Church Row in 1873 and thirty-nine years later, when he was living at Cannon Hall, his daughter Daphne spent much of her childhood here.

Into humbler circumstances were born the Harmsworth sons, both to be ennobled, and who lived in their youth in the Vale of Health in Hunt Cottage. The future Lord Northcliffe began making real money when he published his magazine called *Answers* from the attic of his house at No. 31 Pandora Road, West Hampstead, though, by all accounts, this would not

have been Northcliffe's choice of an address on which to put a blue plaque. In 1890, with his brother Harold (the future Lord Rothermere), he founded *Comic Cuts* and, six years later, the *Daily Mail*.

Good for many newspaper stories, but slightly before the Harmsworths could write them, was Lillie Langtry, actress and mistress of Edward VII when he was Prince of Wales. She lived at Leighton House in Alexandra Road, where twelve gallons of milk were delivered on Thursdays for a weekly bath.

The building of Fitzjohn's Avenue and the adjoining roads from 1876 brought in prosperous people but few notable artists. Frank Holl, portrait painter, was at Three Gables, No. 6 Fitzjohn's Avenue in the 1880s, and the architect R. Norman Shaw lived in his own building at No. 6 Ellerdale Road. He also built the original Moreland Hall, a house in Netherhall Gardens and also No. 61 Fitzjohn's Avenue, for a now-forgotten artist, Edward Long. Shaw's best-known client in Hampstead was the children's writer and illustrator Kate Greenaway, who commissioned him to design the splendid No. 39 Frognal in 1885; here she continued a sad and fruitless romance with John Ruskin, mostly by correspondence. His unfortunate attitude towards women was to claim her a victim as well. She died here in 1901.

Hampstead's reputation for housing people who espouse uncommon or unpopular causes is a 20th-century one, but certainly Annie Besant, whose enthusiasms in the late 19th century included socialism and theosophy, and a much-publicised relationship with Charles Bradlaugh the MP, would have suited the later Hampstead notoriety. Besant lived here while she prepared for her trial, in which the offence was her publication of a booklet advocating birth control. She was found guilty, sentenced to imprisonment and released on a technicality. Marie Stopes, family-planning pioneer, was at No. 14 Well Walk in 1909 and spent her disastrous first marriage at this address. Sigmund Freud, still widely derided by his colleagues, fled Vienna with his daughter

*91. Sir Rowland Hill.*

*92. George du Maurier.*

109

Anna in 1938 and lived for just over a year in Hampstead just before his death.

The Edwardian age, that odd description for the thirteen years before the 1st World War, was the culmination of a growing division between privileged and poor. Such inequality was already being challenged, at first by those born with money, such as Annie Besant, and then by people like Ramsay MacDonald, born poor in Scotland, voted into Parliament by 1906, and made leader of the Labour Party by 1911. He lived at No. 9 Howitt Road from 1916 until 1925, and was here when he formed the first, short-lived Labour government in 1924. In 1925 he moved to the much more sumptuous No. 105 Frognal, Flitcroft's old house. Some of his colleagues were none too happy about his residence in one of the most prestigious suburbs in London, a disgruntlement endured by several Labour Party leaders since. Certainly Hampstead had a needling effect on those socialists who did not live there, even in those days. George Bernard Shaw, who was fortunate enough to be married to a millionairess, had no good opinion of Hampstead: '. . . no money for any good cause can be raised in Hampstead.' He described it as 'the most hopelessly damned centre of callous suburbanisation on earth'.[5] It is from about this time, although MacDonald was not the inspiration, that the leftist nature of Hampstead's famous residents became noticeable.

An exhibition at the Camden Arts Centre in 1974 which depicted Hampstead artists in the 1930s was subtitled, aptly, *A Committed Decade*. The art movements of the late 19th and early 20th centuries had some political basis, but many of the artists living in Hampstead in the 1930s were overtly political, as well as having revolutionary attitudes towards their arts. A committed socialism was shown in the work of painters, sculptors, writers, philosophers, film-makers, architects and musicians. The practitioners included Moore, Hepworth, Nicholson, Gabo, Kokoschka, Gertler, Mondrian, Maxwell Fry, Gropius and Spender.

Most lived or worked in or around the Mall Studios, seven modest buildings off Parkhill and Tasker Roads erected by architect Richard Batterbury in 1872 to be leased as working studios: they were not intended as residences, although they became so later on.[6] Batterbury, who had a particular interest in building for artists, erected Steeles Studios and houses for 'gentlemen artists' in Hampstead Hill Gardens.[7] The early users of the studios, but who lived elsewhere, included artists such as James Linton and Robert McBeth, who resided in Parkhill Road. George Clausen, the painter, was a resident in 1879, and painter Cecil Stephenson records in his notebook that he took over his studio at No. 6 in 1919 from Sickert. Generally speaking, though, the early group of artists, mainly painters of large landscapes, are mostly forgotten now.

The Modern Movement artists arrived first in the late 1920s and were then augmented in the thirties by refugees from the political and social upheavals on the Continent. Henry Moore was one of the first, living at No. 11a Parkhill Road where he was near to his friend Barbara Hepworth, who had moved into No. 7 Mall Studios with her first husband John Skeaping. It was here that Hepworth first produced a 'pierced-hole' sculpture, and here that her marriage capsized and her long affair and marriage with Ben Nicholson began.

Hepworth and Nicholson were founding members in 1933 of Unit One, a collective group of artists and architects formed by Paul Nash, who lived in Eldon Grove. This group was largely superseded in 1935 by Circle, another collective which espoused modern architecture and abstract and constructivist art. Naum Gabo, the Russian constructivist artist, was a member, and he lived nearby in what were known as the Isokon flats in Lawn Road. These flats, built in 1934, were a landmark in modern English architecture. Isokon, derived from the words 'Isometric Unit Construction' was largely the brainchild of designer Jack Pritchard and architect Wells Coates. Special furniture, utilising the versatility of plywood, was designed for the flats and, indeed, Pritchard conceived of the Isokon formula being repeated in houses and flats elsewhere, using furniture based on the same principles. In effect, the apartments were fully furnished, leaving the tenants free to come and go lightly; this was part of the philosophy of Isokon, which wanted people to be rid of 'permanent tangible possessions' so as to enjoy travel and new experiences.[8]

The influence of the Modern Movement on the Continent, represented by such architects as Le Corbusier, Gropius and Lubetkin, was at work here. Architecture, previously regarded as indulgent and only occasionally functional, was to be, for this group, a way of bringing dignity, cohesion and organised function to a new society. The needs of the day, not the styles of the past, were the architect's guide, and these were to be seen in the light of a vision of a classless society. Thus, one concept of town-planning was born in time for the opportunities of post-war Britain.

Another architectural group, called MARS, was formed at the same time, meeting at Pritchard's house in Belsize Park Gardens. One member was Maxwell Fry, whose 1935 Sun House at No. 9 Frognal Way is still required viewing for architectural students; another was Colin Lucas who, with Connell and Ward, produced No. 66 Frognal in 1938. This building, hailed at the time as 'the greatest abortion ever perpetrated', is now regarded as one of the best domestic buildings of that period.

Just as the architects aimed to correct the wrongs and abuses of society by reorganising our physical environment so the literary lions of Hampstead spelt out their ideas. They were more precisely political, especially Stephen Spender, the poet. Others, too, were disenchanted by the politics of the era and hopeful of what was happening in Russia, but they shrank from the political orthodoxy of Spender. These writers included Geoffrey Grigson, the poet and frequent visitor to the Mall Studios, and Orwell, who lived briefly over Westrope's bookshop, where he worked, at the junction of Pond Street and South End Green. But Orwell's friends in Hampstead were mainly political rather than artistic. He described Spender as a 'parlour Bolshevik' until he met him and retracted.[9]

Mark Gertler, born in Spitalfields of Polish parents, was an early member of the Mall Studio group. He lived at a number of Hampstead addresses, including Penn Studio, Rudall Crescent. The group was further enlarged by a stream of innovative artists from Europe: Piet Mondrian installed himself in a small room at No. 60 Parkhill Road, which he painted white and then covered with his vibrant squares and rectangles; Oscar Kokoschka came to England in 1938 and lived first in a ventriloquist's flat in King Henry's Road; Walter

Gropius came soon after the Nazis closed the Bauhaus and Erno Goldfinger, another architect, built Nos. 1–3 Willow Road – three houses which raised a local uproar; he lived in No. 2 himself. Later, artist Fred Uhlman and his wife Diana in Downshire Hill took in John Heartfield, the German who helped to found the Dadaist movement and invented 'montage'; he came for two weeks and stayed with the Uhlmans for five years.

A catalyst amongst all these artists was the ubiquitous Herbert Read, distinguished poet and critic, who lived at No. 3 Mall Studios. He was an arbiter and an historian, who held a position of influence as editor of the *Burlington Magazine*. More importantly, he was the articulate voice of the avant-garde. Not only was he involved with the Mall Studios, he was also a friend of the artists who visited No. 47 Downshire Hill, where the Carline family lived. These included Stanley Spencer who, in 1924, took a studio over the Vale of Health Hotel and here painted his huge *Cookham Resurrection* which is now in the Tate, and who married Richard Carline's sister, Hilda. Roland Penrose lived nearby at No. 21 Downshire Hill. He and Paul Nash were instrumental in the staging of the first international Surrealist exhibition in London. Artists such as Ernst, Arp and Magritte came over for the exhibition and visited No. 21. Robert Bevan, painter of several canvasses depicting Belsize Park where he lived, was a Carline friend as well.

The Downshire Hill artists were politically left. Carline was chairman of the Artists' International Association and from his house, after the Uhlmans took over, the Artists' Refugee Committee functioned in aid of artists displaced by Hitler. But the 'leftness' did not have the same edge as that of the group at the Mall Studios. It was, in Downshire Hill, more a frequent gathering of like-minded friends rather than a group which aimed to radically change the arts and society in general.

[1] See pp. 37–9.
[2] Joseph Farington, Diary, 1803, Vol. 2.
[3] See Thomas J. Barratt, op. cit., Vol. 2, pp. 147–65, and *Keats House Official Guide*.
[4] See the most convincing suggestion in Alan Farmer's *Hampstead Heath* p. 149 (1984).
[5] *Hampstead and Highgate Express*, 4 June 1932.
[6] *The Architect*, 7 August 1872.
[7] Gwen Barnard, 'A Nest of Gentle Artists', *Camden History Review*, No. 8.
[8] See article by Alastair Grieve in catalogue for *Hampstead in The Thirties: A Committed Decade* (1974).
[9] Bernard Crick, *George Orwell: A Life* p. 243 (1980).

## CHAPTER TEN

# Endeavours Crossed by Wars

The 20th century brought new brooms to London when the new borough councils began in 1900. These authorities had extra powers and statutory duties and the optimism which usually accompanies an uplift of status. Sixty-five years later, when Camden was formed, the same sort of feeling transcended the carefully guarded cynicism of party politics.

The sluggish Hampstead Vestry of 1856 had, in the later part of the century, been transformed into a relatively active one. It incurred debts for such things as municipal offices, town improvements, open spaces and a new cemetery, of a size to make the careful tradesmen blanch. To a large extent this was due to the leadership of Sir Henry Harben, president also of the Prudential Assurance Company, but valuable financial and professional help was available from the much-maligned Metropolitan Board of Works and its successor, the London County Council.

The Vestry Hall, baths and washhouses have already been mentioned, but also established was a base for public works or road repairs on the disreputable brickfield between the Midland and Hampstead Junction Railways west of Finchley Road. The Vestry was not too far behind the leaders in London in opening a public library – the first in a converted house at No. 48 Priory Road, in 1895. A second branch was opened in 1897 in Antrim Grove and here the Vestry decided to economise by not using an architect, a decision paid for by the later borough council of 1937 when they had to rebuild it.[1] Harben subscribed £5000 to build the Central Library at the corner of Finchley Road and Arkwright Road in 1897, one year after the Vestry had bought the 8000-volume collection of Professor Henry Morley which formed the basis of the reference library. The old town was not provided with a free library. No doubt it was thought that the Hampstead Subscription Library met the demand, or else that free libraries were somehow inappropriate for the wealthier citizens of the village area. Subsequent schemes to provide one around the High Street seem to have had their inspiration in the dreams of either librarians or councillors rather than in public demand, for they have always come to nought without too much disappointment being expressed.

The Vestry, although not known for its radical views, adopted in one respect a course of municipalisation then being advocated by such groups as the Fabians. In 1894 it rejected the overtures of private supply companies and established its own electricity-generating station at Lithos Road, in the public works yard. In this the Vestry followed the example of St Pancras, the first London authority to use new powers, because they were persuaded that profit would ensue from the investment – it rarely did.[2]

93. *Workmen laying the electricity mains in Gayton Crescent, 1905. Contrary to the wording on the tent they were then employed by Hampstead Borough Council.*

94. *Sir Henry Harben.*

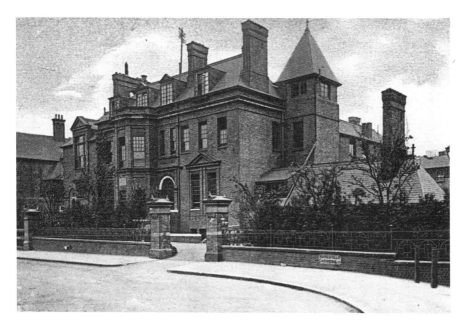

*95. Yorkshire Grey Yard, looking from the tavern. Demolished 1886.*

*96. South Hampstead High School. Postcard c.1906.*

By the time of Harben, influence had slipped away from the almost exclusive hold of the town centre people, and when the Vestry was reformed in 1873 so that vestrymen represented each ward, this trend was hastened. New ecclesiastical districts, formed when churches were well attended, also helped to create a feeling of a Hampstead larger than the old village boundaries.

It was a time for civic pride in buildings, not least in schools for which the Vestry had no responsibility. Implementation of the 1870 Education Act was gathering speed and by 1890 there were four large London School Board buildings in the parish. But prosperous middle-class Hampstead was mainly a place for private schools. Heath Mount School at the top of Heath Street, was founded in 1817 by the Rev. J. Duncan. Its advertisement for 1824 proclaimed that young gentlemen were 'genteely boarded and expeditiously qualified for the various trades and professions'. Fourteen private schools, very small affairs, are noted in a street directory for 1826, in the Hampstead area. Constable sent his daughters to a school on the site of the High Hill Bookshop in the High Street in the 1830s;[3] a school existed in the same position as early as 1762, run by Mrs Russell.[4]

One man who was a scholar at Heath Mount in 1865 recalled that the day consisted of study 7–8 am, breakfast, study 9 am–12 noon, dinner, study 2–5 pm, supper, study 7–9 pm. Half holidays were allowed on Wednesdays and Saturdays. Each boy had to possess an Eton suit and silk hat.[5] The school, which moved to Hertfordshire in 1933–4, numbered Cecil Beaton and Evelyn Waugh among its pupils before the First World War. Its building is shown in illustration 75.

Henley House School, established in the 19th century in Mortimer Crescent, had some distinguished names attached to it. By 1874 the headmaster was J. V. Milne (father of A. A. Milne, who was born here). H. G. Wells, who taught here in 1889, described it as a 'not very successful private school in Kilburn', and A. A. Milne remembers Wells in turn as 'not a great schoolmaster. He was too clever and too impatient.' The Harmsworth children, including the future Lord Northcliffe, were also pupils.[6]

The South Hampstead High School for girls was opened as the St John's Wood High School (trading on the greater prestige of that area's name) in Winchester Road in 1876 before transferring to its splendid building in Maresfield Gardens in 1882. The Hall School for girls was run by the Misses Allen and Olney in 1889 at No. 18 Buckland Crescent and was successful enough to add a new building in Crossfield Road the following year; in 1905 it was bought out by the Belsize School for boys and gradually it became boys only. The Haberdashers' Aske School was moved from the congestion of the City to the comparative rurality of Hampstead in 1898 and here it stayed until 1961 when it leaped further into the countryside of Elstree, to be replaced by the Hampstead Comprehensive School. King Alfred's School was founded in the same year, 1898, in Ellerdale Road, before transferring to North End Road in 1921.

The most famous import was University College School. This institution was founded in a house in Gower Street in 1830 as a 'feeder' for the College itself. It had, as two of its principles, the absence of religious teaching and of corporal punishment, which attracted the description of 'no God and no rod'. It flourished until the 1880s, when the prosperous middle classes began to move to the suburbs and a day-school in the centre of town was not convenient for them. So the junior school moved out to Hampstead, to Holly Hill in 1891, where new premises were built on the site of a Tudor building in 1927; the main school followed in 1907 to a handsome building in Frognal designed by Arnold Mitchell, which was erected with some difficulty over the Westbourne river and on soil made insecure by the presence of additional material dumped there from excavations for the Midland Railway.

The borough was formed as political parties were becoming more evident at local level, although as Hampstead was overwhelmingly middle-class there was no danger of the Conservatives losing control. Under one name or another they controlled the borough council and George Balfour was the sitting member from 1918 to 1941. Despite this, Hampstead was one of the first councils in London to erect working-class flats. In 1905–6 Park Dwellings, in Garnett Road, were built in three blocks. After that the borough's efforts in municipal housing were rare, though not unusually so for a middle-class area with a low population density. The South End Close flats were built in the 1920s, using up the last part of Pickett's old farm, and the Westcroft estate in Cricklewood was begun in 1936 when the council felt that no development was possible within the borough boundaries.

The Hampstead Conservatives date themselves from a meeting in April 1835 presided over by the vicar, which formed the Hampstead Conservative Association to uphold the constitution and to oppose the separation of State and Church. The Vestry Clerk was also a member.[7] The Liberals were prominent much later, though how radical they were is open to research given that the *Hampstead and Highgate Express* criticised them, in 1877, for being happy to recruit from the lower classes but intent on having only gentry and suchlike on their executive committee.[8] The Liberal Association opened new headquarters at No. 24 Heath Street in 1890,[9] and the Labour Party began a branch in town in 1918 with an office in Heath Street ten years later.[10]

Meetings of suffragettes are noticed frequently in the columns of the local papers and although hayricks on Hampstead Heath were set on fire in 1913 by women intent on public demonstration, Hampstead itself does not seem to have been a hotbed of suffragette activity. Despite this a number of residents were associated with early breakthroughs in female emancipation, of whom Besant and Stopes have already been mentioned. When the first women jurors were sworn in at the Old Bailey in 1921, nearly all of them lived in Hampstead,[11] and they were presumably chosen on the assumption that, being educated, they would have a man's judgement. Westfield College, under the redoubtable management of Constance Maynard, founded for 'the higher education of women on Christian principles', was established in two houses in Maresfield Gardens in 1882 before it moved to Kidderpore Hall.

A Hampstead woman was also instrumental in the promotion of the Fabian Society. Charlotte Wilson, who had been educated at Newnham College, Cambridge, moved into Wyldes farmhouse in the hope that she might live off her own endeavours on the smallholding rather than on the income of her stockbroker husband. E. Nesbit, the children's writer, recalls her 'farmhouse'

*Overleaf:*
*97. Wyldes, North End. From a watercolour by A. R. Quinton, 1910.*

117

A.R.QUINTON

kitchen here, for all the world like the ones in recent fashion, with aesthetic pots, pans, curtains and furniture. Charlotte Wilson founded, *c*.1884, a society which met in her house and which had the misleading name of the Hampstead Historic Club. It actually discussed politics, free love and social reform, and quite a few of its members also belonged to the newly-formed Fabian Society. Frequent attenders at Wyldes therefore included George Bernard Shaw, Olive Schreiner, Havelock Ellis, Sidney Webb and Ernest Rhys. They also discussed *Das Kapital* without much unison. Shaw described their discussions of this work, which was not yet available in English:

> A young Russian lady used to read out 'Capital' in French to us until we began to quarrel which usually occurred before she had gone on long enough to feel seriously fatigued. The first chapters were of extraordinary efficacy in getting us by the ears . . . The controversy raged at Hampstead until Bax shook the dust of the heath off his boots, and the Historic Club, having had enough of impassioned disputes as to whether the value of Mrs Wilson's vases was fixed by the labour socially necessary to produce them, by their cost of production on the margin of cultivation, or by the final utility of the existing stock of vases, insisted on passing to the later chapters and dropping the subject.[12]

It was no wonder that Mrs Wilson turned to anarchism later. However, it was at Wyldes that the famous *Fabian Essays in Socialism* were fashioned and it was these which put the Society in the public eye.

Utopian visions were halted by the First World War. The call to patriotism to help in this rearrangement of the map of Europe had its consequences in Hampstead as well:

> Often seen in Hampstead, during World War One were telegraph boys, riding bicycles, and wearing their distinctive caps, who were busy delivering telegrams, informing the wives and relatives of men at the front, that their men folk were killed, or missing in action. People dreaded seeing these boys cycling down their road, and they fearfully peeped through their windows, hoping that the boy would not knock on their front door, and hand them the fateful telegram.[13]

Army hospitals were opened, such as in Rosslyn Lodge, Lyndhurst Road, or in Cedar Lawn, North End Way. Some rationing was introduced, some residents with German names were intimidated, and some air-raids occurred.

Destruction of Hampstead's old buildings however, as after the Second World War, was principally a peace-time occupation. The age of mansion flats arrived and the Hampstead of large family houses with their abundant retinues of servants was over. Part of Church Row was an early casualty in 1898, when Gardnor Mansions were commenced. So was the house called The Pryors on East Heath Road, which was superseded by two overbearing blocks in 1902–3 designed by Hall and Waterhouse. But mostly the apartment blocks were products of the 1930s. On the site of Thomas Barratt's old house, Bellmoor, was built the block of flats with the same name, rented out at from £750 per annum. In Haverstock Hill, near the Underground station, a great deal of Belsize Park was transformed by rows of flats from 1934, and when the New College at Swiss Cottage was sold the same year it, too, was replaced by flats. In the High Street the Greenhill block was commenced in 1935. People who had old houses, even famous ones, had problems in selling them. Romney's house on Holly Bush Hill, owned by architect Clough Williams Ellis, failed to reach its reserve price of £12,500 in 1931 and only got to £7500.

*Opposite:*
*98. Heath Street.*
*Postcard.*

*99. Keats House.*
*Postcard.*

*Overleaf:*
*100. The Whitestone Pond, with Bellmoor and Gangmoor, 1910. From a watercolour by A. R. Quinton.*

HAMPSTEAD: HEATH STREET.

HAMPSTEAD: KEAT'S HOUSE, KEAT'S GROVE.

A.R. QUINTON

(He did not sell it, eventually, until 1948.) Ivy House, just outside Hampstead in North End Road, the former home of Pavlova, realised only £15,000 when £19,000 was hoped for in 1932.

Another development of this period was Frognal Close, built by E. L. Freud on the site of a fantasy building called Frognal Priory. This extraordinary place, seen in illustration 73, was erected piecemeal by a retired auctioneer called John Thompson who had acquired the sobriquet of 'Memory Corner Thompson' from winning a bet that he could repeat from memory the name of every corner public-house in a certain part of London. The house, built in the 1820s, had Norman, Early English, Tudor and Gothic features, and contained a collection of elaborate and fanciful artifacts and items of furniture – some of them fakes. He regularly opened the house for curious members of the public to visit. Thompson died in 1836 and his niece, a Mrs Gregory, inherited. She was married to an unscrupulous publisher who let the house go to ruin and plundered its contents. The Gregories then disappeared leaving the house empty. Twenty three years later an old widow called Grummitt who, with her late husband had been caretakers, claimed ownership of the crumbling house. However, as no heir had appeared since the Gregories' departure it had reverted to the lord of the manor and he evicted the widow much to the disgust of a public meeting in 1876 called to support her cause. The house was demolished soon after.

Elsewhere, amid much protest, the old Norway House off the High Street was cleared away to make way for a garage and petrol station known later, in the 1970s controversy, as the Blue Star site. At the top of Heath Street, with the demolition of the old Upper Heath/Flask, Lord Leverhulme built the Queen Mary Maternity Home. One landmark did escape, though, when in 1921 the purchase of Keats House was completed, with largely American money. This was opened to the public in 1925 and the Heath branch library next door, built in 1931, housed the Keats Memorial Library. The seclusion of the street was nearly ruined in 1899 when the London School Board announced a plan to take over four houses opposite Keats House and build a school there.[14]

Households became smaller, more compact. The vast houses of the 19th-century estates were broken up into flats and single rooms and, for a time, Hampstead began to deteriorate in the condition of its houses and their facilities, and in the regard of potential house purchasers. Professional people, the backbone of the Hampstead economy, moved out instead to places made accessible by the car and the Underground.

The traders had to adapt to this altered situation. They dealt now not with the household servants but with the household owners, and also faced retail competition which threatened their livelihood. Small shopkeepers have a love-hate relationship with the multiples in that the latter take most of the trade but attract enough people to the locality to provide sufficient profit for the minnows. So the town shopkeepers probably welcomed the advent of Boots, Woolworth's and Sainsbury's at the top of the High Street. But they would not have been happy about the opening of the John Barnes department store in 1900, complete with the use of eight houses behind for staff quarters, because it dragged trade away to Finchley Road; the store was rebuilt in 1936

101. *Advertisement for Joseph Lane, chemist of No. 29 High Street.*

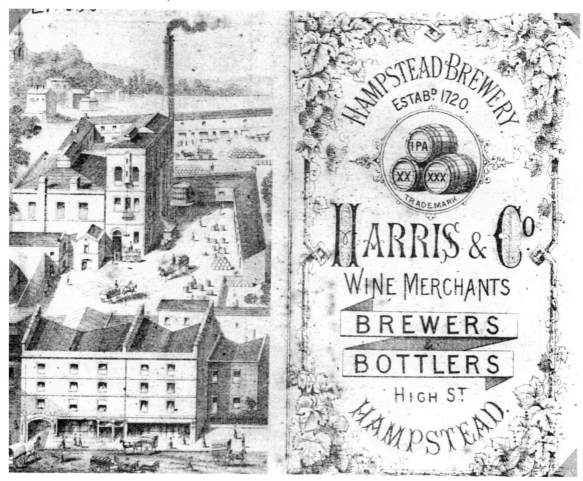

*102. Advertisement for Hampstead Brewery.*

by T. P. Bennett. Finchley Road, however, has never fulfilled its promise as a shopping street. One side of it has remained virtually without shops and the other has failed to attract more than a handful of multiples, and now the traffic makes it unpleasant. B. B. Evans, another department store, opened in Kilburn High Road in 1897.

Except in more recent times the Hampstead shops in the old town have been for the local population – it is the current complaint of residents that most of them now are not. There were exceptions, of course, such as the jewellers Knowles-Brown, founded in 1891, which had a wider reputation and warranted a longer journey; this business closed on Christmas Eve, 1984. The old family businesses almost outlasted John Barnes but they, too, were swept away by market forces at roughly the same time. G. H. Gaze, the drapers at Nos. 65–6 High Street for many years, went in 1980, Forsters, the grocers which could trace its history back to 1774, went late in 1979 and Fowlers, the ironmongers at No. 40 High Street, closed the same year.

One business to thrive as the estates multiplied was the Hampstead Brewery off the bottom of the High Street. It was founded in 1720 by John Vincent, whose son, by the 1760s, supplied or owned the Three Tuns, the

White Hart and the Black Boy and Still at least, and also had another brewery on the site of the junction of Hampstead High Street and lower Heath Street.[15] By 1928 the Brewery had 184 employees but the business was gone by 1932.

The efforts to extend the Heath before and after the beginning of the 20th century are indications of a community taking its town and scenery seriously. The Hampstead Heath Protection Society was formed in 1897, initially to save the Heath from its owners, the London County Council, who seemed intent on turning the Heath into a municipal park. Nine years earlier an organisation called the Northern Heights Footpath Association was formed to preserve the footpaths of Hampstead and the neighbourhood.

Issues of the day were discussed at the Hampstead Parliamentary Debating Society. Established in 1883 and still functioning in the 1960s, this forum of residents, initially divided between Conservatives and Liberals, went through the motions of appointing a Prime Minister and other ministers of national importance, and conducted serious debates with the tight-lipped politeness and jolly heckling which they hoped would be appropriate at Westminster.

There was a surge of interest in local history in the same period which stemmed from the publication of *Records of Hampstead*, edited by F. E. Baines, a vestryman who helped to establish the electricity generating station, and who was to be appointed Assistant Secretary of the General Post Office. The Hampstead Antiquarian and Historical Society had its first meeting in 1898, largely through the efforts of C. J. Munich. It published its *Transactions*, but a more useful publication for local historians was the *Hampstead Annual*, begun in 1897 by Sydney Mayle, printer and publisher of Hampstead and Clerkenwell, and edited by Ernest Rhys. These fairly sumptuous volumes were published until 1907. One of the active members of the Society was G. W. Potter, who wrote a number of useful publications including one on Hampstead Wells, and whose father established a building business in Hampstead which became the well-known estate agency.

The Hampstead Scientific Society arose out of the free availability of a 10½-inch reflecting telescope in 1899. P. E. Vizard, a keen astronomer, led a group of local residents into forming the Hampstead Astronomical and General Scientific Society, which persuaded the LCC to provide a site for the telescope by Hampstead Ponds. Within a year there were 192 members, of which 49 were women.[16] Lectures ranged over general and natural science as well as astronomy. In 1909 the observatory near Whitestone Pond was established.

Music was also organised in Hampstead. In 1878 a Dutch pianist and composer called William Coenen formed the Hampstead Choral Society.[17] Another centre of activity was Burgh House where Thomas Grylls, a noted stained-glass artist, held frequent musical events. Longer-lasting was the Hampstead Conservatoire, housed in a building on the site of the Embassy Theatre at Swiss Cottage by 1894, complete with a Willis-built organ. Cecil Sharp, who helped to revive a nationwide interest in folk dance and song, was its director from 1896 until 1905. The Conservatoire did not outlast the 1920s and the Embassy Theatre was there by 1929, only to begin a precarious existence itself. It limped along until wartime, was bought by Sidney Bern-

*103. The Hampstead
Scientific Society's
Observatory near
Whitestone Pond.
From a drawing by
A. R. Quinton 1911,
reproduced from
Barratt's* Annals of
Hampstead *(1912).*

*104. Hampstead
Conservatoire, Swiss
Cottage. Postcard
c.1905.*

*Opposite:
105. The entrance to
Flask Walk in June
1903. The bridge
rooms collapsed in
1911 and were not
replaced.*

HAMPSTEAD HEATH. JACK STRAWS CASTLE & WAR MEMORIAL..

*106. The War Memorial erected after the 1st World War by Jack Straw's Castle. Postcard.*

stein in 1953 for productions of experimental plays, and was sold out quickly to the Central School of Speech and Drama in 1956.

More conventional theatres were the Kilburn Empire and Kilburn Palace. The Empire, in Kilburn High Road, opened in 1906 with shows twice nightly. The Palace began in 1886 at Nos. 254–6 Belsize Road in a building with the grandiose name of the Kilburn Town Hall; this was designated the Theatre Royal, Kilburn ten years later and it became a cinema in 1909.[18]

The Everyman Theatre began in the old Drill Hall at Holly Bush Vale in 1920 with few funds, much optimism, helpful assistance from the LCC, and Norman MacDermott as director. Its most famous production was *The Vortex* in 1924, written, produced and starred in by Nöel Coward. One actress resigned because of his 'studied rudeness' and Lord Cromer, whose duties included theatre censorship, objected to a reference to two young ladies going away together. He said that it implied they might be lesbians. Confronted with this the amused Coward said, 'If only I had thought of that myself.'[19]

The Everyman was an important theatre between the wars. Eugene O'Neill was presented for the first time and actors of the calibre of Mrs Patrick Campbell, Edith Evans, Carleton Hobbs, Ellen Terry and Claude Raines all appeared here. Despite that, it folded in 1931.

It was not until 1933 that Jim Fairfax-Jones, lawyer turned cinema buff, opened his cinema in the same building, specialising in foreign films. It was a brave enterprise which needed lengthy nursing. His wife Tess ran the Foyer Gallery where Paul Klee was given his first public show. Since then the cinema has become part of the fabric of Hampstead.

It is claimed that the first moving pictures shown in Hampstead were at Frederick Gray's fairground in the Vale of Health, using a hand-held projector.[20] The first cinema appears to have been the Hampstead Picture Palace at No. 64 Heath Street, at the corner with Back Lane. In its six years, from 1910, it was also known as the Eldorado, and it was then converted into a tea room.[21] The Frognal Bijou Picture Palace opened in 1911 in Finchley Road opposite the Midland railway station. Even the attraction of free afternoon teas did not prevent its demise in 1922. The Playhouse (now the Classic), in South End Green, replaced Hereford House in 1913, and when it was converted to 'talkies' in 1930 it still retained a full orchestra to accompany the supporting film. T. P. Bennett designed the Odeon in Haverstock Hill in the 1930s, and in the confident days of cinema expansion the large Odeon at Swiss Cottage was opened in 1937.

*107. The Hare and Hounds, North End.*

The principal local newspaper, the *Hampstead and Highgate Express*, responded to the new societies, churches and shops by increasing its size to eight pages in 1902. But the onset of the Second World War brought a diminishment of advertising and a financial crisis loomed with the Jealous family unwilling or unable to fund the paper's survival. The business was already a primitive one. John Parkhurst, who was editor and wrote most of the paper from 1932, recalled that when he first joined it in 1921 it possessed no guillotine: readers had to cut the pages themselves. The office had no typewriter either, so that all copy and business letters were written by hand. These elementary pieces of equipment were not bought until after 1932. The paper moved to Perrins Court later in the 1930s and the old flat-bed printing

108. One of the last
rockets to fall in
London badly damaged
the Hampstead
Central Library,
Arkwright Road.
Photograph 1945.

machine was replaced by a rotary press, but money was still desperately short.

During the war, John Parkhurst engineered its sale, on a personal basis, to S. Goss, a director of the printing firm Baines & Scarsbrook. Goss kept it going through the war years and his nephew, Arthur Goss, recalls that when he worked as its manager in Perrins Court, he was responsible not only for the administration and much else besides, but also for delivery of copies to the newsagents in the early hours of Friday mornings.

Generally the content was of local interest only, but the exception was the column written in the years prior to the Second World War by 'Augur' which commented on national events. 'Augur's' real name was Vladimir Poliakoff, a Russian emigrée journalist who had high-level connections in the Italian government. He was, in fact, used by Chamberlain as a go-between in his dealings with Italy during the period when Chamberlain hoped that Italy would have a moderating effect on Hitler and so prevent a war. Poliakoff, part of the comings and goings of appeasement, was therefore in favour of such a policy in his weekly column, but he changed his mind, or appeared to, when Hitler invaded Czechoslovakia in 1939.[22]

The first significant air-raid over Hampstead occurred on 9 September 1940, when two houses in Upper Park Road were destroyed and one person killed. The total number of missiles logged as falling on the borough during the entire war included 286 high-explosive bombs, 2500 incendiary devices and 10 flying-bombs. Casualties numbered 930 and deaths totalled 204.[23] Undoubtedly these would have been higher if, in the biggest raid of all, on 10/11 May 1941, all thirteen of the high-explosive bombs which fell on Hampstead had not failed to explode. The library at Westbere Road was destroyed in 1941, and the Central Library at Arkwright Road damaged by bombs in 1940 and 1945. The large old houses behind Jack Straw's Castle were so badly damaged that they were never rebuilt and the land, fortuitously, was added to the Heath in 1952. Other notable casualties were Pitt House at North End and the nearby Hare and Hounds public house, but the worse-hit area was West Hampstead, which contained the complex of railway lines.

[1] Christopher Wade, ed., *More Streets of Hampstead*, p. 45 (1973).
[2] Professor F. M. L. Thompson, op. cit., p. 413.
[3] Christopher Wade, *The Streets of Hampstead*, p. 67 (1984).
[4] James Ellis, 1762 map of Hampstead.
[5] E. V. Knox, *The Adventures of a School* (ND).
[6] Christopher Wade, ed., *The Streets of West Hampstead*, p. 43 (1975).
[7] *Hampstead and Highgate Express*, 26 January 1895, p. 5, which reprinted the original convening notice.
[8] Ibid, 3 February 1877.
[9] Ibid, 16 June 1890, p. 6f.
[10] Ibid, 27 September 1968 and 15 December 1928.
[11] Ibid, 15 January 1921.
[12] Quoted in Philip Venning, *Wyldes, A New History*, p. 13 (1977)
[13] Memories of Hugh Turpin published in *Wartime Camden* (1983) by the London Borough of Camden.
[14] *Hampstead and Highgate Express*, 11 November 1899.
[15] James Ellis, 1762 map of Hampstead.
[16] Anon., *Seventy-Five Years of Popular Science*, Record of the Hampstead Scientific Society, 1899–1974 (1974).
[17] Jerry and Elizabeth Shields, 'Musical Hampstead', *Camden History Review*, No. 2.
[18] Diana Howard, *London Theatres and Music Halls 1850–1950* (1970).
[19] Norman MacDermott, *Everymania: The History of the Everyman Theatre, Hampstead, 1920–26* (1976).
[20] Mary Leigh, Merry-go-round in *The Heathside Book*, ed. Ian Norrie (1962).
[21] Christopher Wade, *The Streets of Hampstead*, p. 59. (1984).
[22] Information ex Michael Benaim.
[23] *Hampstead at War 1939–45*, repr. Camden History Society.

# CHAPTER ELEVEN

# The Whole becomes one-third

In 1951 the Church Commissioners were persuaded to sell parts of their Belsize estates because it was predicted that they would go down in status and value. A wry smile at this advice from Messrs Cluttons, the well-known surveyors and valuers, is all very well, but who could have foretold the resurgence of demand for older property, not just in Hampstead, but in depressed areas like Kentish Town and Islington. The increasing cost of flats and houses has governed to a large degree the character of Hampstead since the last war. As values have gone up so have rents and rates, and general retailers with high stock levels and moderate profit margins have been forced out; houses have been sub-divided and their divisions again divided, the tenants tossed about between market forces and government intervention loose enough to be circumvented, but which in the end encouraged higher rents.

It has not been a comfortable era for those with memories of Hampstead at a slower pace. Their household shops have disappeared to be replaced by businesses seemingly unrelated to their ordinary existence, although the survival of Stamp's, the chemist, is welcome. On the credit side is the tenacious expansion of Ian Norrie's High Hill Bookshop, which has done much to create a new social focus in the High Street. Mr Norrie, renowned for his dislike of official notices on the Heath, objectionable children and opticians occupying shops in prime positions, has also done much to make local history publishing less of a gamble.

Traffic now moves incessantly up the High Street to gouge through narrow Holly Hill and Heath Street. Restaurants attract an evening trade, so there is no break, no sundown quiet, no halt to the stream of visitors. It began with the coffee-bars, a phenomenon of the 1950s, which obliged the Heath and Old Hampstead Society to press for a restriction of their numbers. Young people in duffle-coats eked out cups of coffee and risottos in inexpensive places like El Serrano's in Heath Street, and bought the *Hampstead and Highgate Express* early on Friday mornings to look for bed-sitting rooms – there were, then, columns of them. The presence of this slightly bohemian population had its attractions, and even the less adventurous sought it out; soon prosperity and respectability crept down the slopes of Hampstead again. This happened only in Hampstead village and, to a lesser extent, in Belsize. West End and Kilburn, administratively part of Hampstead, were worlds away in life-style the characteristics of which had hardly changed since between the wars, excepting a larger immigrant population.

Before 1945 the Borough Council had been dominated by the Ratepayers'

*109. Swiss Cottage 1964.*

Association and the Municipal Electors' Association, the latter, in theory, eschewing party politics altogether. The labelled politicians were the few Labour Party representatives who were first returned in Kilburn ward in 1937, but from 1945 the Hampstead Conservative Association nominated and sponsored candidates under its own banner. From that date they dominated the Council.

Yet, as in the 1930s, Hampstead was the home of left-wing causes, or, at least, causes which were identified with the left. Arthur Goss, proprietor of the *Hampstead and Highgate Express*, together with Sheila Jones of the Hampstead Labour Party, founded what became the Campaign for Nuclear Disarmament in the late 1950s, and the Hampstead branch was its largest and most influential. Sidney Silverman, a Labour MP who lived in Finchley Road, led the campaign to abolish capital punishment; his campaign secretary was Peggy Duff, who was later to be a St Pancras councillor and secretary of CND. In 1957, Roy Shaw, secretary of the Hampstead Labour Party, promoted David Pitt as the Labour Party's choice at the next general election – the first black candidate in British politics. This selection caused controversy in his own party, as well as nationwide interest, for it was thought that Pitt would lose the working-class vote of Kilburn; in the event, his vote was quite respectable. Dr. Pitt went on to become the first black member of the House of

*110. Swiss Cottage
Library.*

Lords. The local Labour Party was also in the national headlines after sections of it mounted a campaign to depose Hugh Gaitskell as Party leader following his adamant opposition to unilateral disarmament.

But it also has to be said that for all the lively discussion at Labour Party Town ward meetings, it was a party bereft of local power. Its only representatives on the Council were from Kilburn and there was, in the memory of several veterans of those days, a healthy antipathy between Kilburn and Town ward members. The Borough Council in the eyes of the activists of Town ward had not the importance it has today, because their political endeavours were concentrated on national issues. But for Kilburn members, the Council was an important instrument by which that area's deficiencies might be remedied.

The Council built a number of large-scale housing developments after the war, such as those in Well Walk, Parkhill Road, King Henry's Road and West End Lane, and a huge development was begun at Abbey Road before Camden took over. By the 1960s the Council was involved with Max Rayne in the redevelopment of the Eton College Chalcot estate between King Henry's Road and Fellows Road; also, schemes were afoot in Netherwood Street, Palmerston Road and Alexandra Road, where a private development had aroused so much opposition that the Borough Council was persuaded to take it over.

The main development controversies, not all of them political, revolved around four sites – Swiss Cottage, the Royal Free Hospital, the Blue Star site and Branch Hill.

In the 1950s the purple-brick St Dunstan's School for the Blind and the St Columba's Hospital were removed from Swiss Cottage; this enabled the Council to think about developing the whole island site. The architect residents of Hampstead pressed for something bold and modern and the Council, in some quandary, considered and discarded the idea of a competition. It was Leslie Room, leader of the Conservatives, who persuaded them to appoint Basil Spence as architect – he was then riding on the reputation of his Coventry Cathedral. Only two of his buildings, the library and the baths, were built. Mercifully, a tower with a heliport on the roof got no further than an idea, and Hampstead's MP, Henry Brooke, acting in his ministerial capacity, delayed permission to build the civic and administrative blocks because of spending restrictions. When times were more propitious the merger with Camden was imminent and the Civic Centre was shelved, leaving the eyesore carparks and corrugated iron to remain until quite recent times.

*111. James Roose-Evans in the rehearsal room of the Hampstead Theatre Club at the Three Horseshoes, c.1959. Photograph by Helen Craig, kindly supplied by James Roose-Evans.*

137

One organisation caught up in the indecision over this site was the Hampstead Theatre Club. James Roose-Evans began the theatre in the Moreland Hall in 1959 with professional but virtually unpaid actors. They rehearsed at the Three Horseshoes where the upper room was, at one time, to be their auditorium had it been adaptable to the fire regulations. In founding this 'fringe' theatre at a time when few people knew the meaning of the term, Roose-Evans was renewing a Hampstead tradition begun by the Everyman and followed by the Embassy. The Club was obliged to leave the Moreland Hall and in desperation turned to Hampstead Council who, by 1962, provided them with a shell of a building on the Swiss Cottage site leaving the Club to find £10,000 with which to furnish it. The Theatre opened in December 1962 with a production of Chekov's *The Seagull* but there were several financial crises in the next eight years; it is doubtful if it would have survived had not (Sir) Max Rayne paid off its £10,000 debts in 1963. In the same year the Theatre had its first major success with a revival of Coward's *Private Lives* and followed it with the premier of *Cider With Rosie*. From this year the Theatre's reputation was established but even by 1964 they were still living very frugally: the entire wage-bill for all the non-acting staff that year was £116.00 a week, which included the £15 paid to James Roose-Evans.

The original wooden shell was regarded as a temporary home and in the days when there were grandiose ideas for the Swiss Cottage site it was fully expected that a new, permanent, theatre would be built there. Instead, and fortuitously, the old building has been added to and moved, and it has escaped the civic theatre transformation.

The Royal Free Hospital opened in 1974 on the sites of two older establishments. Its monstrous size and uninspiring aspect, which have spoilt many views from the Heath, were the butt of much opposition. Unfortunately the hospital authority did not require the permission of the Council to build, only its observations. The scheme was given permission at ministerial level.

Similar worry was caused by the proposed redevelopment of the Blue Star site in the High Street. The unsightly gap in the building façade needed a handsome in-filling, but with what? Proposals came and went, all much criticised, and Hampstead was lucky that the *Hampstead and Highgate Express* ran a spirited campaign against schemes which had more to do with profit than with architecture. Despite this, a complex of buildings has been erected which is at odds with the High Street façade.

The Branch Hill Lodge dispute was a political one. As early as 1953 the Communist Party in Hampstead advocated that the house and grounds be compulsorily purchased and 900 council dwellings put on the site. It was a time of severe housing shortage and a touching faith in tower blocks. In St Pancras the leader of the Council, John Lawrence, was pressing the same course for Fitzroy Park or Witanhurst. By the early 1960s the matter was being discussed in earnest as the owner, Lord Glendyne, was inclined to sell. Hampstead did not have much of a housing-list – indeed, with the acquisition of dwellings in the redeveloped Chalcots estate it was hoped that all the 500-odd applicants for housing would be absorbed. So Branch Hill was not even a candidate for council homes, although some Conservatives were keen

to see it added to the Heath while others were content that it should be privately developed. The advent of Camden changed the situation entirely. Suddenly the housing waiting-list was enlarged by the desperate numbers of St Pancras and Holborn. All at once Branch Hill became an opportunity for genuine housing gain, for there were few other virgin sites in the rest of the borough. After Camden had completed purchase a housing development was announced. Accusations of betrayal followed, because it was alleged that the vendor had been given a personal assurance (not included in the sale agreement) that the site would not be developed in such a way. Further controversy was caused by the eventual cost of the buildings, due principally to the difficulties posed by the site.

In one controversy the two main parties agreed. An Inner London motorway was proposed which would have cut a great swathe through Hampstead, principally through the Chalk Farm area, in a tunnel and over-ground. It is difficult to believe now that this scheme could ever have been realised, but it seemed threatening enough at the time. The renowned and best abilities of the Hampstead lobbyists were displayed in a prolonged campaign and the plan was eventually shelved, although hints as to its resuscitation are given now and then.

*112. Branch Hill Lodge, 1899.*

*113. The Isokon flats, Lawn Road, 1985. Photograph courtesy of the* Hampstead and Highgate Express.

*114. Modern buildings in Maryon Mews by Ted Levy, Benjamin and Partners. Photograph by Horst Kolo, courtesy of the architects.*

The White Paper containing proposals to reform London government was published in 1961. It suggested an amalgamation of Hampstead, St Pancras and Holborn, and despite several counter-proposals, such as a Hampstead merger with St Marylebone, a St Pancras link with Finsbury and Shoreditch, and a Holborn amalgamation with Westminster, the original plan was adhered to.

*115. No. 49a Downshire Hill, by Michael Hopkins. By kind permission of the* Architects' Journal.

The Hampstead Conservative Party was divided on the matter. It was used to local power and feared that it would lose it in the new arrangement; a good number still felt that party politics should be kept out of local government, and the prospect of a liaison with a socialist St Pancras, which was rarely out of the headlines, was not encouraging in this respect. Generally speaking, the younger Conservatives were interested in the challenge of what most thought was a borough they could win if Holborn was included, whereas the older members were reluctant bedfellows. It has been contended that all the parties to the merger saw the new borough as marginal but certainly the St Pancras Labour Party was not keen, not only because it was concerned at the abolition of the LCC and the likelihood of a Conservative GLC, but because it was sure that in most borough elections in Camden the Conservatives would have a majority. On the other hand, the Hampstead Labour Party was in favour of Camden because it was sure to bring them more municipal experience.

The Hampstead Conservatives were shaken when, in fact, the Labour Party won the first Camden election in 1964 with a slim majority, and even more so when, in a sensational election in 1966, Ben Whitaker won the Hampstead Parliamentary seat from Henry Brooke – the only time the Conservatives had lost control. It was a traumatic period for the Tories in Hampstead and Leslie Room stepped down from leadership of the Council group. He was replaced by Geoffrey Finsberg, who in 1968 led the Conservatives to victory in the Council elections and who, in 1970, wrested back the Parliamentary seat for the Conservatives.

The reluctant Hampstead Tories had been correct – Camden, from the beginning, was a highly political borough at both Council and staff levels. International, national and local problems all found their way on to Council agendas and the friendly, but wary, relationship between the two main political parties evident in the 1960s, deteriorated. This is properly the subject of a larger study, but it is interesting that the new hard edge in Council politics was accompanied by a bolder commentary on local affairs in the Hampstead and Highgate Express. This newspaper was sold to Home Counties Newspapers in 1964 and has since benefited from a securer financial base, the quite remarkable increase in estate-agency advertising, and the introduction of new technology such as computer typesetting in 1984 and colour printing in 1985. Gerald Isaaman, its editor since 1968 and only its sixth since Jealous bought the paper in 1862, has steered the paper away from a former polite radicalism to hold a left-of-centre position. It has done much, also, to further the aims of local artists and societies.

When the new central library opened at Swiss Cottage the old building at Arkwright Road became redundant. Demolition was briefly considered, as the old structure was thought to be unsafe after war damage. Instead, an arts centre was established here, the result of an unusual partnership of local authority, arts organisation and education authority. Crucial to this arrangement was the well-established Hampstead Artists' Council, led by Jeannette Jackson and Bernard Gay, who had exhibition experience and numerous

*116. The Royal Soldiers' Daughters' Home. Postcard c.1905. The remaining part of this building was demolished in 1970.*

visual arts contacts, and who were able to obtain a grant from the Inner London Education Authority to run an art school here. The Artists' Council was founded in 1944 by Richard Carline as a regional society of his Artists' International Association. In its early days it had temporary premises in the home of the poet William Empson and organised art classes at Burgh House; in 1953 it began the Open Air Art Exhibition at the top of Heath Street.

Two other well-known properties came into prominence. Fenton House was bequeathed to the National Trust by Lady Binning in 1952. Thus, the oldest house in Hampstead came into the public domain together with its contents. Burgh House, ten years younger (built 1703), was already a community centre, having been bought by Hampstead Council soon after the last war, but Camden had no use for it. The Burgh House Trust was formed and in 1979 took over the house to use for meetings, exhibitions and a local history museum. By then, local history was a thriving business, a phenomenon cynically attributed to the insecurity of modern life or the increase in leisure time. Whatever the reason, it brought into existence the Camden History Society in 1970.

The conservation debate rages frequently in Hampstead. The older, more picturesque houses of the town are now so well guarded, at least against demolition, that it is difficult to imagine any more of them disappearing, unless by some illegal action. Legislation has helped, but Hampstead has been particularly fortunate in its watchdog, the Heath and Old Hampstead Society, whose main preoccupation at the time of writing is the future administration of the Heath after the abolition of the GLC.

The complaint of modern architects is that areas like Hampstead can become ossified, with change rejected for the sake of it. They can point, with justification, to some very good modern buildings in the borough. These include Kingswell and Maryon Mews by Ted Levy, Benjamin and Partners, Old Brewery Mews by Dinerman, Davison and Partners, Chaim Schreiber's old house in West Heath Road, designed by James Gowan in 1963, and, Michael Hopkins' stunning glass structure in Downshire Hill. Earlier, in 1970, there was Peter Clapp's new shopfront for Drazin's in Heath Street. It can be done, yes, but the insensitive way in which parts of Belsize, Fitzjohn's Avenue, Swiss Cottage and the Vale of Health have been treated urges more caution than courage.

It is a dilemma for planner and architect, for whom it used to be customary in the 1960s to think in terms of the replenishment of housing stock within sixty years or so. As Hampstead reaches its one thousandth recorded year many of its properties have stood for at least a fifth of that span and are now protected in perpetuity. How long will it be before the formal but homely and pleasant terraces of Belsize and Chalcots are thought of in the same way? The question must be asked: is this what we want?

APPENDIX ONE

# Notable Residents of Hampstead

Printed below is a list of notable people who have lived in Hampstead. It was prepared in a very short time and in a period when the appropriate rate books were unavailable. It is therefore presented as no more than a basis for future research and in the hope that readers will contribute towards its revision and enlargement. It does not include people still alive.

The principal sources are the *Hampstead and Highgate Express* and *The Streets of Hampstead* series edited by Christopher Wade.

AGATE James Evershed (1877–1947)
Drama critic.
22 Antrim Mansions.
10 Fairfax Road 1939.

AIKIN Lucy (1781–1864)
Writer.
8 Church Row late 1790s and early 1800s.
Buried Hampstead churchyard.

AKENSIDE Mark (1721–1770)
Poet and physician.
Golders Hill House 1747–50.

ALLINGHAM Helen (1848–1926)
Painter.
Eldon House, Eldon Grove 1880s.

ALLINGHAM William (1824–1889)
Writer.
Eldon House, Eldon Grove, 1874–89.

ALVANLEY Lord (1745–1804)
(Richard Pepper Arden)
Lord Chief Justice.
Frognal Hall, Church Row

ASQUITH Herbert H. (1852–1928)
Prime Minister.
12 Keats Grove 1877–87
27 Maresfield Gardens 1887–92

AUMONIER James (1832–1911)
Painter
84 Fellows Road 1885–86.
162 Adelaide Road 1897–1900.
The Studio, Eton Villas 1903.
5 Wychcombe Studios, Englands Lane 1904

AYRES Ruby M. (1883–1955)
Writer.
48 Arkwright Road 1939.

BAILLIE Joanna (1762–1851)
Writer.
Church Row 1785.
Bolton House, Windmill Hill *c.1791–1851*.

BAIRD John Logie (1888–1946)
Television pioneer.
84 Lawn Road *c.1932*.

BALCHIN Nigel (1908–70)
Writer.
Marlborough Mansions, Cannon Hill.

BALOGH Lord Thomas (1905–1985)
Economist.
Well Walk.
14 Hampstead High Street 1971–80.

BARBAULD Anna Letitia (1743–1825)
Writer.
8 Church Row *c.1791*.
Heddon House, Rosslyn Hill 1801.

BARNETT Dame Henrietta (1851–1936)
Founder of Hampstead Garden Suburb.
Heath End House, Spaniards Road 1889–.

BARRATT Thomas (1841–1914)
Hampstead historian.
Bellmoor House on site of flats in East Heath Road 1877–1914.

BAX Sir Arnold (1883–1953)
Composer.
Ivy Bank, Haverstock Hill 1896–1911.
155 Fellows Road 1st World War–1941.

BEATON Cecil (1904–80)
Photographer.
Born 21 Langland Gardens.
1 Templewood Avenue 1911–22.
Scholar at Heath Mount School.

BECKFORD William (1709–70)
Lord Mayor of London.
West End House, West End Lane.

BEECHAM Sir Thomas (1879–1961)
Conductor.
7 Bellmoor, East Heath Road 1939.

BEECHEY Sir William (1753–1839)
Painter.
Upper Terrace.
Rosslyn Hill.
155 Haverstock Hill.

BEERBOHM Sir Max (1872–1956)
Writer and cartoonist.
12 Well Walk 1st World War.

BENJAMIN Arthur (1893–1960)
Composer.
15 Ranulf Road.

BENTLEY Edmund Clerihew (1875–1956)
Writer.
28 Lymington Road 1920s.

BERNAL Professor J. D. (1901–71)
Physicist.
35 Downshire Hill 1930s.
60 Clifton Hill 1939.

BESANT Annie (1847–1933)
Social reformer and theosopher.
17 Mortimer Crescent 1877.

BESANT Sir William (1836–1901)
Historian.
12 Gayton Crescent.
18 Frognal Gardens 1893–1901.
Buried Hampstead churchyard.

BEVAN Robert (1865–1925)
Painter.
14 Adamson Road 1901–25.

BLAKE William (1757–1827)
Poet and engraver.
Stayed at Wyldes, North End in 1820s.

BLISS Sir Arthur (1891–1975)
Conductor.
1 East Heath Road 1929–39.

BLOMFIELD Sir Reginald (1856–1942)
Architect.
51 Frognal.

BOMBERG David (1890–1957)
Painter.
10 Fordwych Road 1930–33.
66a Lymington Road 1937.
17 Greville Place 1939–40.
Rosslyn Hill.
Steeles Road.

BONE Stephen (1904–58)
Painter.
43 Haverstock Hill until 1938.
Died at 140 Haverstock Hill.

BONHAM-CARTER Lady Violet (1887–1969)
Politician.
Born 12 Keats Grove.

BOULT Sir Adrian (1889–1983)
Conductor.
41 Avenue Close, Avenue Road 1939.
Compayne Gardens 1977.

BOYDELL Josiah (1752–1817)
Engraver.
West End Lane *c.1782–c.1806*.

BRAIN Dennis (1921–57)
Horn player.
37 Frognal.

BRIGHOUSE Harold (1882–1958)
Writer.
67 Parliament Hill 1919–58.

BROWN Ford Madox (1821–93)
Painter.
Heath Street 1852.
Hampstead High Street.
12 The Mount 1883.

BROWN Ivor (1891–1974)
Drama critic.
Hampstead Hill Gardens.
20 Christchurch Hill for nearly 50 years.

BUSS Frances Mary (1827–84)
Pioneer of women's education.
Myra Lodge 87–9 King Henry's Road 1869–94.

BUTT Dame Clara (1873–1936)
Singer.
Compton Lodge, 7 Harley Road 1900–29.

CAMERON James (1911–85)
Journalist.
Eton College Road.

CAMPBELL Mrs. Patrick (1865–1940)
Actress.
Pitt House, North End Avenue 1922.

CARLINE Richard (1896–1980)
Artist.
47 Downshire Hill

CHAMPNEYS Basil (1842–1935)
Architect.
Hall Oak, Frognal 1881.

CHRISTIE Dame Agatha (1890–1976)
Writer.
Isokon flats, Lawn Road.

CLARK Sir Kenneth (1903–1983)
Art historian.
Capo di Monte, Windmill Hill.
Upper Terrace House, Upper Terrace.

CLAUSEN Sir George (1852–1944)
Painter.
4 Mall Studios *c.1879*.

COBDEN-SANDERSON Thomas (1840–1922)
Craft bookbinder.
49 Frognal 1890s.

COCKERELL Charles Robert (1788–1863)
Architect.
Ivy House, North End.

COLE Sir Henry (1808–82)
Organiser of the 1851 Great Exhibition and public official.
3 Elm Row 1879–80.

COLLINS Sir Norman (1907–82)
Writer and broadcaster.
Mulberry House, Church Row.

COLLINS Wilkie (1824–89)
Writer.
Born North End.

COLLINS William (1788–1847)
Painter.
North End 1823.
Pond Street 1826–30.
20 Avenue Road 1839–40.

COLVIN Sir Sidney (1845–1927)
Keeper of prints and drawings at British Museum, and art critic.
Abernethy House, Mount Vernon.

COMPTON Fay (1894–1978)
Actress.
22 Well Walk 1929.

CONSTABLE John (1776–1837)
Painter.
Albion Cottage, Upper Heath 1820.
2 Lower Terrace 1821–22.
Stamford Lodge, Heath Street 1823.
25–26 Downshire Hill 1826.
40 Well Walk 1827–37.
Buried Hampstead churchyard.

COOPER Dame Gladys (1888–1971)
Actress.
35 Elsworthy Road 1939.

CRAIG Edward Gordon (1872–1966)
Artist and stage designer.
8 Downshire Hill early 1900s.

CRAIK Mrs. Dinah (1826–87)
Writer.
Wildwood Cottage, North End 1857–63.

DALE Sir Henry (1875–1968)
Physiologist.
Mount Vernon House 1919–42.

DANBY Thomas (1816–86)
Painter.
1 Squires Mount 1843–47
21 Downshire Hill 1848.
Glydder House, Haverstock Hill 1855–66.
44 Upper Park Road 1869–82.

DAVIES Sir Henry Walford (1869–1941)
Composer.
21 Fawley Road 1901–11.

DAVIES Margaret Llewellyn (1861–1944)
Social reformer.
28 Church Row 1920s.
26 Well Walk 1926–35.

DE GAULLE Charles (1890–1970)
President of France.
99 Frognal 1940–2.

DE LASZLO Philip (1869–1937)
Painter.
3 Fitzjohns Avenue 1922–37.

DELIUS Frederick (1862–1934)
Composer.
4 Elsworthy Road end 1st World War.
Belsize Park Gardens.

de MORGAN William (1839–1917)
Ceramic artist.
91 Adelaide Road 1855.

DICKENS Charles (1812–70)
Writer.
At Wyldes for a few weeks in 1837.

DICKSEE Sir Frank (1853–1928)
Painter.
3 Greville Place 1920s.

DOBSON William (1817–1898)
Painter.
Adelaide Road.

DRINKWATER John (1882–1937)
Writer.
10 Belsize Square 1921–22.
North Hall, Mortimer Crescent 1934–37.

DUFFERIN Lady (1807–67)
Poet and lyricist.
Pavilion Cottage, Vale of Health 1850s.

du MAURIER George (1834–96)
Artist and writer.
4 Holly Mount 1869.
27 Church Row 1870–74.
28 Hampstead Grove 1874–95.

du MAURIER Sir Gerald (1873–1934)
Actor.
Born 27 Church Row.
28 Hampstead Grove 1874–95.
Cannon Hall, Cannon Place 1916–34.

EDWARDS John Passmore (1823–1911)
Philanthropist and newspaper proprietor.
51 Netherhall Gardens 1908–11.

ELGAR Sir Edward (1857–1934)
Composer.
Severn House, site of Nos. 42–44 Netherhall Gardens
1912–21.

ELLIS Sir Clough Williams (1883–1978)
Architect.
Romney's House, Holly Bush Hill 1929–.

EMPSON William (1906–1984)
Writer.
160 Haverstock Hill 1940.
Hampstead Hill Gardens 1946.

ERSKINE Lord (1750–1823)
Lord Chancellor
Erskine House, Spaniards Road 1788 for 33 years.

FABER Sir Geoffrey (1889–1961)
Publisher.
1 Oak Hill Park 1930s.

FARJEON Eleanor (1881–1965)
Writer.
20 Perrins Walk 1920–.

FERRIER Kathleen (1912–53)
Singer.
97 Frognal 1942–53.

FIELDS Dame Gracie (1898–1979)
Variety artist.
Gardnor Mansions, Church Row 1930s.
20 Frognal Way 1934.

FLEMING Ian (1908–64)
Writer.
Pitt House, North End Avenue in youth.

FLITCROFT Henry (1697–1769)
Architect.
105 Frognal 1740s and 1750s.

FOLEY John Henry (1818–74)
Sculptor.
Priory, Upper Terrace 1874.

FREUD Anna (1895–1982)
Psychoanalyst.
20 Maresfield Gardens.

FREUD Sigmund (1856–1939)
Psychoanalyst.
39 Elsworthy Road Jun–Jul 1938.
20 Maresfield Gardens 1938–1939.

FRY Roger Eliot (1866–1934)
Artist.
22 Willow Road 1903–*c.1908*.
Pond Street.

GABO Naum (1890–1977)
Artist.
101 Cholmeley Gardens, Fortune Green Road 1938–9.
101 Mill Lane 1939–46.

GAITSKELL Hugh (1906–63)
Labour Party leader.
18 Frognal End.

GALSWORTHY John (1867–1933)
Writer.
Grove Lodge, Admirals Walk 1918–33.

GARNETT Richard (1835–1906)
Archivist and writer.
27 Tanza Road 1899–1906.

GARVIN James Louis (1868–1947)
Editor of The Observer.
9 Greville Place.

GERTLER Mark (1891–1939)
Painter.
Penn Studios, Rudall Crescent 1915–26.
19 Worsley Road 1926–30.
22 Kemplay Road 1932.
53 Haverstock Hill 1933–36.
Pilgrims Lane.
1 Wellmount Studios 1932–33.

GIBBERD Sir Frederick (1908–1984)
Architect.
49 Downshire Hill.

GILLIES Margaret (1803–87)
Painter.
25 Church Row 1862–87.

GOODALL Frederick (1822–1904)
Artist.
62 Avenue Road (studio) 1902.
36 Goldhurst Terrace 1902–4.

GRANT Duncan (1885–1978)
Painter.
143 Fellows Road 1905–6.

GREENAWAY Kate (1846–1901)
Writer.
39 Frognal 1885–1901.
Buried Hampstead Cemetery.

GREENWOOD Lord Anthony (1911–82)
Politician.
38 Downshire Hill.

GREENWOOD Arthur (1880–1954)
Labour leader.
Gainsborough Gardens.

GROPIUS Walter (1883–1969)
Architect.
3 Wildwood Terrace late 1930s.
15 Isokon flats, Lawn Road.

HAMMOND Barbara (1873–1961)
Social historian.
Hollycot, Vale of Health 1906–13.

HAMMOND John Lawrence le Breton (1872–1949)
Social historian.
Hollycot, Vale of Health 1906–13.

HARKER Gordon (1885–1967)
Actor.
6 Lyndhurst Road.
Gloucester House, Downshire Hill.
45 Belsize Avenue.

HARMSWORTH Alfred (1865–1922)
(Lord Northcliffe)
Newspaper proprietor.
Rose Cottage (now Hunt Cottage),
Vale of Health 1870.
94 Boundary Road *c.1874–*.
99 South End Road 1880s.
37 Sheriff Road 1885.
77 Iverson Road *c.1887*.
78 West End Lane.
31 Pandora Road 1888–91.
Scholar Henley House School, Mortimer Crescent.

HARMSWORTH Harold (1868–1940)
(Lord Rothermere)
Newspaper proprietor.
Rose Cottage, (now Hunt Cottage), Vale of Health 1870.
94 Boundary Road *c.1874–*.
Wedderburn Cottage, Wedderburn Road.
Pitt House, North End Avenue 1905–8.

HASSALL Christopher (1912–63)
Writer.
Old Cottage, Vale of Health 1954–59.

HEARTFIELD John (1891–1968)
Painter.
47 Downshire Hill (1938–50).

HENGLER Charles (1820–87)
Circus proprietor.
27 Fitzjohns Avenue.
Buried Hampstead Cemetery.

HEPWORTH Dame Barbara (1903–75)
Sculptor.
2b Pilgrims Lane.
7 Mall Studios 1927–39.
3 Mall Studios 1934–39.

HILL Octavia (1838–1912)
Social reformer.
Pond Street in childhood.

HILL Sir Rowland (1795–1879)
Postal reformer.
East Heath Road 1848.
Pond Street 1848.
Bartrams, Hampstead Green 1849–79.

HOARE John Gurney (1810–75)
Banker and leader of fight to save Hampstead Heath.
The Hill, North End Way.

HOGARTH William (1697–1764)
Painter.
Building on site of Bull and Bush, North End Way, when young.

HOLIDAY Henry (1839–1927)
Painter and sculptor.
Oak Tree House, Redington Road 1875–1920.
18 Chesterford Gardens 1921–27.

HOLL Francis (1845–88)
Portrait painter.
Scholar at Heath Mount School and University College School.
6 Fitzjohns Avenue 1880s.

HOLL William (1807–71)
Engraver.
174 Adelaide Road 1870–71

HOPKINS Gerard Manley (1844–89)
Poet and priest.
9 Oakhill Park 1852.

HUNT James Henry Leigh (1784–1859)
Poet and essayist.
West End Lane area 1812.
Vale of Health 1815–19.
Vale of Health 1820–21.

HUTCHINSON Geoffrey (1893–1974)
(Lord Ilford)
QC and politician.
12 Church Row.

HUXLEY Aldous Leonard (1894–1963)
Writer.
16 Bracknell Gardens 1917–19
18 Hampstead Hill Gardens 1919.
31 Pond Street 1963.

HUXLEY Sir Julian (1887–1975)
Scientist.
31 Pond Street 1943–75.

HYNDMAN Henry M. (1842–1921)
Socialist writer.
13 Well Walk.

JEALOUS George F. (1833–1896)
Proprietor of Hampstead and Highgate Express.
Vale of Health.

JEROME Jerome K. (1859–1927)
Writer.
Byron's Cottage, Vale of Health.
Kilburn Priory.

JOAD Professor Cyril (1891–1953)
Philosopher and writer.
4 The Gables, Vale of Health 1923–24.
4 East Heath Road.

JOHNSON Dr Samuel (1709–84)
Lexicographer and writer.
Stayed at Priory Lodge, Frognal 1748.

KEATS John (1795–1821)
Poet.
Well Walk 1817–18.
Lawn Bank, Wentworth Place (Keats House, Keats Grove).

KING Philip (1904–1979)
Playwright.
44 Fortune Green Road 1950s.

KLEIN Melanie (1882–1960)
Psychoanalyst.
42 Clifton Hill 1939.
16 Bracknell Gardens 1950s.

KNIGHT Charles (1791–1873)
Publisher and social reformer.
Vale of Health 1831.
7 Eldon Grove 1864–70.

KNOX E. V. (1881–1971)
Poet and editor of Punch 1932–49.
34 Well Walk 1922–45.
110 Frognal 1945–71.

KOKOSCHKA Oskar (1886–1980)
Painter.
Mandeville Court, Finchley Road 1938.
King Henry's Road.

LAMB Henry (1883–1960)
Painter.
Vale of Health Hotel 1912–14.

LANGTRY Lillie (1852–1929)
Actress.
Leighton House, Alexandra Road.

LAWRENCE D. H. (1885–1930)
Writer.
1 Byron Villas, Vale of Health 1915.
Heath Street 1923.
1 Elm Row 1923.
32 Well Walk 1917
30 Willoughby Road 1926.
Rudall Crescent.

LEVERHULME Lord (1851–1925)
Industrialist.
The Hill, North End Way (now Inverforth House).

LEWIS John (1836–1928)
Department store founder.
Spedan Tower, Branch Hill 1888–1928.

LINNELL John (1792–1882)
Painter.
Hope Cottage near Bull and Bush 1822.
Old Wyldes 1824–28.

LINTON Sir James (1840–1916)
Painter.
60 Park Road.
7 Mall Studios 1872–79.
35 Steeles Road.
4 Mall Studios 1914–17.

LLOYD Marie (1870–1922)
Variety artist.
98 King Henry's Road 1906.

LONGMAN Thomas Norton (1771–1842)
Publisher.
Greenhill, Hampstead High Street.

LOVELL G. W. (1804–78)
Dramatist.
18 Lyndhurst Road.

LOW Sir David (1891–1963)
Cartoonist.
Studio at 13a Heath Street 1939

LUTYENS Elisabeth (1906–1983)
Composer.
13 King Henry's Road 1960s.
Belsize Park Gardens 1960s.

LYND Robert W. (1879–1949)
Journalist and essayist.
14 Downshire Hill.
5 Keats Grove 1930s.

LYND Sylvia (1888–1952)
Poet.
14 Downshire Hill.
5 Keats Grove 1930s.

McBETH Robert (1848–1910)
Painter.
62 Park Road 1873–74.
Studio at 6 Mall Studios 1875–79.
2 Wychcombe Studios 1880–84.
42 Loudoun Road.

MacDONALD Ramsay (1866–1937)
Prime minister and Labour Party Leader.
9 Howitt Road 1916–25.
103 Frognal 1925–37.

MacKENZIE Sir Compton (1883–1972)
Writer.
Woodbine Cottage, Vale of Health 1937–43.
28 Church Row 1910.

MacNEICE Louis (1907–63)
Poet.
4a Keats Grove 1930s.

MALLESON Miles (1888–1969)
Actor.
27 Belsize Square 1939.

MANSFIELD 1st Earl of (1705–93)
(William Murray)
Lord Chief Justice.
Said to have lodged at the Chicken House, Rosslyn Hill in
student days.

MANSFIELD Katherine (1888–1923)
Writer.
17 East Heath Road 1918–21.
6 Pond Street 1922.

MARTIN Kingsley (1897–1969)
Political writer. Editor New Statesman.
4 East Heath Road during 2nd World War.

MASEFIELD John (1878–1967)
Poet.
13 Well Walk 1914–16.

MAY Phil (1864–1903)
Illustrator.
Haverstock Hill.

MONDRIAN Piet (1872–1944)
Artist.
60 Parkhill Road *c.1938–40.*

MONSERRAT Nicholas (1910–79)
Writer.
Isokon flats, Lawn Road.

MOORE Thomas Sturge (1870–1944)
Writer.
40 Well Walk 1930s.

MORISON James Cotter (1832–88)
Essayist.
Holyrood House, Windmill Hill 1880 for 2 months.
30 Fitzjohns Avenue *c.1880–88.*

MORISON Stanley (1889–1967)
Typographer.
11 Holly Place 1919–21.
9 Golden Square (now Mount Square)
1916–19.

MORLEY Professor Henry (1822–94)
Writer.
8 Upper Park Road 1858–.

MUIR Edwin (1887–1959)
Poet.
7 Downshire Hill 1932–35.

MURRY John Middleton (1889–1957)
Writer.
Pond Street.
17 East Heath Road 1918–21.
1a The Gables, Vale of Health 1926.

NASH Paul (1889–1946)
Artist.
3 Eldon Grove 1936–39.

NEALE Edward Vansittart (1810–92)
Christian Socialist and a founder of the Co-operative
movement.
12 Church Row 1881.

NEVINSON C. R. W. (1889–1946)
Artist.
Born Keats Grove.
1 Steeles Studios 1939.

NEVINSON Henry Woodd (1856–1946)
Essayist.
4 Downside Crescent 1939.

NICHOLSON Ben (1894–1982)
Artist.
7 Mall Studios 1931–39.
3 Mall Studios 1934–39.
2b Pilgrims Lane 1973.

NIGHTINGALE Florence (1820–1910)
Nursing reformer.
Oak Hill Park 1859.
3 Upper Terrace Lodge 1860.
3 Oak Hill Park 1862.
7 Oak Hill Park 1864.

ONIONS Oliver (1873–1961)
(George Oliver)
Writer.
Heath House, New End Square.

ORCHARDSON Charles (1873–1917)
Artist.
1 Park Road Studios 1896–98.
54 Parkhill Road 1899–1901.
86 Fellows Road 1902.
3 Wychcombe Studios 1903–4.
54a Parkhill Road 1907.

ORWELL George (1903–50)
(Eric Blair)
Writer.
Above bookshop at corner of Pond Street and South End
Green – No. 3 Warwick Mansions in 1934–35.
77 Parliament Hill 1935.
10a Mortimer Crescent 1944.

PALGRAVE Sir Francis (1788–1861)
Scholar and public archivist.
Tensleys, Hampstead Green 1834–61.

PALMER Samuel (1805–81)
Artist.
Stayed at Wyldes occasionally.
Son-in-law of John Linnell.

PARRY William (1790–1855)
Arctic explorer.
Heath End House, Spaniards Road.

PATMORE Coventry (1823–96)
Married Hampstead parish church 1847.
Elm Cottage, North End 1861.

PATTI Adelina (1843–1919)
Singer.
8 Primrose Hill Road.

PEARSON Karl (1857–1936)
Mathematician and biologist.
7 Well Road.

PENROSE Sir Roland (1900–1984)
Artist and writer.
21 Downshire Hill 1936–39.
36 Downshire Hill post 2nd World War.

PERCEVAL Spencer (1762–1812)
Prime minister.
Belsize House 1797–1807.

PETRIE Sir William Flinders (1853–1942)
Archaeologist.
8 Well Road *c.1901*
5 Cannon Place 1919–35.

PEVSNER Nikolaus (1902–1983)
Architectural historian.
2 Wildwood Terrace, North End 1936–83.

PITT William the elder (1708–78)
(1st Earl of Chatham)
Prime minister.
Stayed in 1767 in a house on the site of the present Pitt House, North End Avenue.

PRIESTLEY J. B. (1894–1984)
Writer.
27 Well Walk early 1930s.

RACKHAM Arthur (1867–1939)
Illustrator.
6 Wychcombe Studios, Englands Lane 1900.
54a Parkhill Road 1903.

RAYMOND Ernest (1888–1974)
Writer.
22 The Pryors, East Heath Road.

READ Ernest (1879–1965)
Musicologist.
40 Marlborough Hill 1939.
Flat 1, 151 King Henry's Road 1960s.

READ Herbert (1893–1968)
Art critic and writer.
3 Mall Studios 1934–35.

REDFERN James F. (1838–76)
Sculptor.
Clifton House, South End Green.

REIZENSTEIN Franz (1911–1968)
Composer.
34 Hollycroft Avenue 1960s.

RHYS Ernest (1859–1946)
Writer and editor.
Hunt Cottage, Vale of Health 1890s.
Hermitage Lane, West Hampstead 1905.

ROBERTSON E. Arnot (1903–1961)
96 and 98 Flask Walk 1950s.
23 Flask Walk.

ROBESON Paul (1898–1976)
Singer.
The Chestnuts, Branch Hill 1930s.

ROLFE Frederick (1860–1913)
Iverson Road 1886.
69 Broadhurst Gardens 1899–1904.

ROMNEY George (1734–1802)
Painter.
6 The Mount 1796.
House now called Romney's House, Holly Bush Hill 1797–99.

ROSENBERG Isaac (1890–1918)
Poet and painter.
32 Carlingford Road 1912–.

ROSSETTI Dante Gabriel (1828–1882)
Painter and poet.
Spring Cottage, Downshire Hill, site of Hampstead Hill Mansions, 1860.

ROSSLYN 1st Earl (1733–1805)
(Alexander Wedderburn)
Branch Hill Lodge.
Rosslyn House.

RUCK Berta (1878–1978)
Writer.
17 East Heath Road.

SCOTT Sir George Gilbert the elder (1811–78)
Architect.
Admiral's House, Admiral's Walk 1856–64.

SCOTT George Gilbert the younger 1839–97)
Architect.
26 Church Row.

SEDLEY Sir Charles (1639–1701)
Poet, dramatist.
Died at what became known as Steele's Cottage, Haverstock Hill.

SELLERS Peter (1925–80)
Actor.
Northwood Lodge, Oak Hill Park.
Feb 1962–Jan 1963.

SELOUS Henry Courtney (1801–90)
Painter.
Wentworth Place (Keats House) 1838.

SHARP Cecil (1850–1924)
Pioneer of folk music and dance.
183 Adelaide Road 1905–11.
27 Church Row 1915–18.
4 Maresfield Gardens 1918–24.

SHAW Martin (1875–1958)
Composer.
18 Belsize Lane.
8 Downshire Hill 1898.
Fortune Green.
Finchley Road.
Parliament Hill.

SHAW R. Norman (1831–1912)
Architect.
Albion Road (now Harben Road) as a boy.
6 Ellerdale Road 1875–1912).
Buried Hampstead churchyard.

SHELLEY Percy Bysshe (1792–1822)
Poet.
Pond Street for a few weeks.

SICKERT Walter (1860–1942)
Painter.
54 Broadhurst Gardens 1885–94.
Possibly 6 Mall Studios pre-1919.

SIDDONS Sarah (1755–1831)
Actress.
Capo di Monte, Windmill Hill 1804–5.

SILVERMAN Sidney (1895–1968)
Politician and campaigner for the abolition of capital
punishment.
122c Finchley Road 1960s.

SILVESTER Victor (1900–78)
Dance band leader.
Boydell Court, Swiss Cottage.

SITWELL Dame Edith (1887–1964)
Poet.
42 Greenhill, Prince Arthur Road 1961–64.
20 Keats Grove Jun–Dec 1964.

SMITH George Murray (1824–1901)
Publisher. Founder of *Cornhill Magazine* and the *Dictionary
of National Biography*
Oak Hill Lodge 1863–72.

SOSKICE Frank (1902–1979)
Politician and Attorney General.
(Lord Snow Hill).
19 Church Row.

SPENCER Herbert (1820–1903)
Philosopher.
64 Avenue Road 1889–97.

SPENCER Sir Stanley (1891–1959)
Painter.
Adelaide Road.
Vale of Health Hotel 1914–27.

SPILSBURY Sir Bernard (1877–1947)
Pathologist.
20 Frognal.
31 Marlborough Hill 1939.

STANFIELD Clarkson (1793–1867)
Painter.
85–88 Hampstead High Street (Stanfield House) 1847–65.
6 Belsize Park Gardens 1865–67.

STEELE Sir Richard (1672–1729)
Essayist, playwright, politician.
Steele's Cottage, Haverstock Hill 1712–13.

STEEVENS George (1736–1800)
Writer and commentator on Shakespeare.
Upper Heath, Heath Street 1771–1800.

STEPHENSON Cecil (1889–1965)
Artist.
6 Mall Studios 1919–65.

STEPHENSON Robert (1803–59)
Civil engineer.
House on site of 145 Haverstock Hill 1835–43.

STEVENS Alfred (1818–75)
Artist.
9 Eton Villas.

STEVENSON Robert Louis (1850–94)
Writer.
Visits to Abernethy House, Mount Vernon 1873–79).

STOKES Adrian (1902–72)
Painter.
Isokon flats, Lawn Road.
Church Row.

STOPES Marie (1880–1958)
Family planning pioneer.
25 Denning Road (girlhood).
14 Well Walk 1909.

SWEET Henry (1845–1912)
Philologist.
188 Heath Street 1879–87.

SWINGLER Stephen (1915–69)
Politician.
6b Belsize Park Gardens.

TAGORE Sir Rabindranath (1861–1941)
Writer.
3 Villas on the Heath, Vale of Health 1912.

TERRY Fred (1863–1933)
Actor.
4 Primrose Hill Road.

TEULON Samuel S. (1812–73).
Architect.
Tensleys, Hampstead Green 1871.

THOMAS Dylan (1914–53)
Poet.
Possibly Parliament Hill 1937.

TOPHAM Francis William (1808–77)
Painter.
43 Adelaide Road 1870.
4 Arkwright Road.

TOPHAM Frank William Warwick (1838–1924)
43 Adelaide Road 1862–68.
28 Studios, King Henry's Road 1869–70.
16 Prince Arthur Road 1878–89.

TREE Sir Herbert Beerbohm (1852–1917)
Actor–manager.
Grange, West Heath Road 1880s.

UNWIN Sir Raymond (1863–1940)
Architect.
Wyldes Farm, 1906–40.

UNWIN Sir Stanley (1884–1968)
Publisher.
4 Oak Hill Park 1940s–68.
Married Lyndhurst Road church.

VANE Sir Henry the younger (1613–62)
Politician.
Vane House, Hampstead High Street.

VON HUGEL Baron (1852–1925)
Theologian.
4 Holford Road 1882–1903.

WADDELL Helen (1889–1965)
Writer and translator.
32 Primrose Hill Road *c.1933–65.*

WALBROOK Anton (1900–67)
Actor.
69 Frognal.
Buried Hampstead churchyard.

WALFORD Edward (1823–97)
Writer and antiquary.
Church Row.

WALLACE Edgar (1875–1932)
Writer.
Vale Lodge, Vale of Health.

WALTON Sir William (1902–83)
Composer.
10 Holly Place *c1939.*

WARE Isaac (?–1766)
Architect.
Frognal Hall 14 Church Row.

WAUGH Evelyn (1903–66)
Writer.
11 Hillfield Road 1903–8.
Scholar Heath Mount School.

WEBB Beatrice (1858–1943)
Socialist writer.
10 Netherhall Gardens 1892–93.

WEBB Mary (1881–1927)
Writer.
Adelaide Road.
12 Hampstead Grove 1923.

WEBB Sidney James (1859–1947)
(Baron Passfield)
Socialist writer.
10 Netherhall Gardens 1892–93.

WEDDERBURN Alexander – see Rosslyn

WELLS Herbert George (1866–1946)
Writer.
17 Church Row 1909–12 (intermittently).

WHISTLER James McNeil (1834–1903)
Painter.
St Judes Cottage, Spaniards Road 1895–96.

WHITEING Richard (1840–1928)
Writer.
35a Hampstead High Street. (Died here).

WILDE Jimmy (1892–1969)
Boxer.
The Cottage, Whitestone Lane 1933–35.

WILKIE Sir David (1785–1841)
Painter.
Lodged for few months 1810 at Bolton House, Windmill Hill.

WISE Thomas James (1859–1937).
Book collector and forger.
23 Downside Crescent 1901–11.
25 Heath Drive 1911–37.

WOLFIT Sir Donald (1902–68)
Actor.
5 Wildwood Grove 1950s.

WOOD Sir Henry (1869–1944)
Conductor.
4 Elsworthy Road.

WOOD Mrs. Henry (1814–87)
Writer.
16 St. Johns Wood Park 1866–87.

WYNYARD Diana (1906–64)
Actress.
104 Hillfield Court, Belsize Avenue 1960s.

ZANGWILL Israel (1864–1926)
Writer.
Church Row.

APPENDIX TWO

# Hampstead Public Houses

The earlier public houses of Hampstead are listed below. The date for each is the first known record, generally taken from the licensing records held at the Greater London Council Record Office.

ANGEL. Location unknown. 1723 only.

BARLEY MOW. Location unknown. 1726 only.

BEAR. See White Bear.

BELL, Kilburn. 1721. Probably 17th century.

BELL AND HORNS, Hampstead High Street. Holdens Directory 1805.

BIRD IN HAND, 39 Hampstead High Street. 1771.

BLACK BOY AND STILL, Hampstead High Street. 1751.

BLACK BULL, North End. 1742 only.

BLACK LION, West End Lane. 1721.

BLACK LION, Kilburn. 1721. Probably 17th century.

BULL AND BUSH, North End. 1721.

CART AND HORSES. See Load of Hay.

CHEQUER. Location unknown. 1721–32.

COACH AND HORSES, 99 Heath Street. 1721.

COCK AND HOOP, West End. 1751.

COCK AND CROWN, Hampstead High Street. 1751.

CROSS KEYS. Location unknown. 1721–23.

CROWN AND THISTLE. Location unknown. 1723–35.

DUKE OF CHANDOS HEAD. Location unknown. 1731 only.

DUKE OF CUMBERLAND'S HEAD, Frognal. 1751–98.

DUKE OF HAMILTON, New End. 1721.

FIGHTING COCKS. Location unknown. 1723 only.

FLASK, Flask Walk. Thought to be *c.1700.*

FOX AND GOOSE. Location unknown. 1726–73.

FREEMASONS ARMS, Downshire Hill. 1819.

GEORGE, Haverstock Hill. 1715.

GREEN MAN (Wells Tavern site), Well Walk. 1735.

HARE AND HOUNDS, North End. 1751.

HAWK, New End Square. 1759.

HOLLY BUSH, Holly Bush Hill. 1807.

HORSE AND GROOM, 68 Heath Street. 1723.

JACK STRAW'S CASTLE, Hampstead Heath. 1713.

KING OF BOHEMIA, Hampstead High Street. 1680.

KINGS ARMS, Hampstead High Street. 1721. Probably 17th century.

KING WILLIAM IV, Hampstead High Street. 1721. Probably 17th century. Previously called the Kings Head.

KINGS HEAD, Pond Street. 1730–35.

LABOURERS ARMS. Location unknown. 1730–31.

LITTLE GREEN MAN. Location unknown. 1774 only.

LOAD OF HAY (previously Cart and Horses), Haverstock Hill. 1721.

MOTHER HUFF'S, Spaniards Road. *c.1678.*

NAGS HEAD, Heath Street. 1698.

NORTH STAR, Finchley Road. 1850.

QUEENS HEAD, Kilburn, 1735–51.

RED LION, Rosslyn Hill. 1751.

RED LION, Kilburn. 1721. Probably 16th century.

SHAKESPEARES HEAD. Location unknown. 1759–65.

SUN. Location unknown. 1756–65.

SWAN, Kilburn. 1732–35.

THATCHED HOUSE. Location unknown. 1721–26.

THREE HORSESHOES, off Hampstead High Street. 1721.

THREE PIGEONS, Frognal. 1723.

THREE TUNS, Hampstead High Street. 1721.

UPPER FLASK, Heath Street. *c.1700.*

WHITE BEAR, New End. 1704.

WHITE HART, Hampstead High Street. 1721.

WHITE HORSE, Kilburn. 1721–26.

WHITE HORSE, Pond Street. 1721.

WINDMILL. Location unknown. 1731–35.

YORKSHIRE GREY, off Hampstead High Street. 1723.

# Select Bibliography

**Manuscript Sources**

Bellmoor Collection, Local History Collection, London Borough of Camden.
Hampstead Manor Court Rolls (extracts).
Hampstead Vestry Minutes.
Hampstead Rate Books.
The 'Feilde Booke' of 1680.
The Heath Keeper's Diary.
Hampstead Parish Registers.
Notes compiled by E. F. Oppé in the Local History Collection.
Licensing records for Holborn Division (Greater London Record Office).


**Maps**

Belsize Manor 1679 (William Gent).
Hampstead Manor 1762 (James Ellis).
Tithe Map of Hampstead 1839.
Hampstead 1814 (Newton. Published in Park's *Topography and Natural History of Hampstead*.
Hampstead 1864 (Daw).


**Published Sources**

Baines, F. E. (ed.), *Records of the Manor, Parish and Borough of Hampstead*, (1890).
Barker, T. C. and Robbins Michael, *A History of London Transport*, Vol. 1, The Nineteenth Century (1975).
Barratt, Thomas J., *The Annals of Hampstead*, (1912).
Barton, Nicholas, *The Lost Rivers of London*, (1962, repr. 1982).
Bentwich, Helen, *The Vale of Health*, (1968, repr. 1977 by Carlile House Press).
*Camden History Reviews* 1–12 (pub. by Camden History Society).
*Camden History Society Newsletters* Nos. 1–91.
Collins, Michael (ed.), Catalogue for *Hampstead in the Thirties: A Committed Decade*, (1974).
Cook, Olive, *Constable's Hampstead*, (1976).
Farmer, Alan, *Hampstead Heath*, (1984).
Fleming, Patricia, *The Educational Provisions for Children of the Lower Orders in the parish of St John's, Hampstead 1850–70 and 1870–1902*, (thesis).
Gee, Christina M., *Hampstead and Highgate in Old Photographs 1870–1918*, (1974).
*Hampstead and Highgate Express*.
*Hampstead Annual*, 1897–1907.
*Hampstead at War 1939–1945*, (1946, repr. by Carlile House Press 1977).
Hampstead Scientific Society, *Seventy Five Years of Popular Science 1899–1974*, (1974).
Holdens *Triennial Directories of London*, 1802, 1805 and 1809.
Howard, Diana, *London Theatres and Music Halls 1850–1950*, (1970).
Ikin, Christopher, *Hampstead Heath Centenary 1971* (1971, revised and republished by High Hill Press 1985 as *Hampstead Heath: The Battle to save it for the public*).
Isenberg, Howard, *A Short History of St Peter's, Belsize Park*, (ND).
Jenkins Simon and Ditchburn, Jonathan, *Images of Hampstead*, (1982).

Jennings, Trevor, *The School in Mill Lane*, (1973).

*Keats House Official Guide.*

Kennedy, J., *The Manor and Parish Church of Hampstead*, (1906).

Knox, E. V., *The Adventures of a School*, (ND) (Heath Mount School).

Lee, Charles E., *Sixty Years of the Northern*, (1967).

Lee, Charles E., *The Horse Bus as a Vehicle*, (1974).

Lee, Charles E., *The Early Motor Bus*, (1974).

Lorimer, D. H., *A Mesolithic Site on West Heath, Hampstead*, (London Archaeologist, Autumn 1976).

MacDermott Norman, *Everymania: The History of the Everyman Theatre, Hampstead, 1920–26*, (1976).

Meller, Hugh, *London Cemeteries*, (1981).

Menear Laurence, *London's Underground Stations: A Social and Architectural Study*, (1983).

*Middlesex Sessions Rolls.*

Newton, E. E., *Fifty Years of Progress in Hampstead 1860–1910*, (1910).

Norrie, Ian, *Hampstead, Highgate Village and Kenwood*, (1977).

Norrie, Ian and Bohm Dorothy, *Hampstead: London Hill Town*, (1981).

Norrie, Ian, ed., *The Heathside Book*, (1962).

Oppé E. F., *Hampstead: A London Town*, (1951).

Park, John James, *The Topography and Natural History of Hampstead*, (1814).

Pocock, John Thomas, *The Diary of a London Schoolboy 1826–1830*, (Camden History Society 1980).

Potter, George W., *Hampstead Wells*, (1904, repr. by Carlile House Press 1978).

Potter, George W., *Random Recollections of Hampstead*, (1907).

Richardson, John, *Highgate: Its History since the Fifteenth Century*, (1983).

Robbins, Michael H., *The North London Railway*, (revised 1983).

Robson, William, *The Government and Misgovernment of London*, (1939).

Rose, Douglas, *The London Underground: A Diagrammatic History*, (ND).

*Rosslyn Hill Chapel: A Short History 1692–1973*, (1974).

*A Short History of St. John's, Downshire Hill, Hampstead, (c.1973).*

Sharpe, Sutton, *Hampstead Heath in 1680 (Hampstead Annual 1904–5).*

Sullivan, David, *Hamlet on the Upgrade (Hampstead and Highgate Express*, 25th May 1979).

Thompson, F. M. L., *Hampstead: Building a Borough*, (1974).

*Transactions of the Hampstead Antiquarian and Historical Society*, 1898–1905.

Venning, Philip, *Sycophant Extraordinary (Hampstead and Highgate Express*, 19 May 1978).

Venning, Philip, Wyldes: A New History, (1977).

Victoria County History volumes on Middlesex.

Wade, Christopher, *The Streets of Hampstead*, (1984).

Wade, Christopher, ed., *More Streets of Hampstead*, (1973).

Wade, Christopher, ed., *The Streets of West Hampstead*, (1975).

*Wartime Camden*, (1983 London Borough of Camden).

*Westfield College 1882–1932.* (1932).

White, Caroline, *Sweet Hampstead*, (1903).

White, H. P., *London Railway History*, (1971).

Wistrich, Enid, *Local Government Reorganisation: The first years of Camden*, (1972).

# INDEX

The entries do not include names in the Appendix.

Abbey Road 136
Abel, James 80
Aberdare Gardens 85
Adelaide Road 79
Admiral's House 44, 108
Agincourt Road 93, 95
Agriculture 24
Ainger, Rev. Thomas 55
Alehouses 22
Alexandra Road 136
Apothecary 37
Arbuthnot, Dr John 31
Arkwright Road 16, 82
Arnold, Christopher 46
Artists' Refugee Committee 112
Assembly Rooms 62, 74
Atye, Sir Arthur 13

Baillie, Joanna 106, 106 (ill)
Baines, F.E. 7, 127
Baines and Scarsbrook 68, 132
Bakerloo line 99
Balchin, Nigel 68
Balfour, George 117
Baptists in Hampstead 57
Barbauld, Anna 103
Barbauld, Rochemont 103
Barnett, Henrietta 77, 78, 77 (ill)
Barracks, Willow Road 60
Barratt, Thomas J. 75 (ill), 76, 78, 120
Barritt, Charles 68
Barton, Admiral 44
Bartrams 66, 108
Bassett, Rowland George 68
Baths and Washhouses 65 (ill), 66, 137
Batterbury, Richard 110
Bax, Arnold 82
Beadles 36, 37
Beaton, Cecil 116
Beauchene, Fitzjohn's Avenue 83 (ill)
Beckford, William 87 (ill), 88
Bell, Kilburn 23, 36 (ill), 36
Bell Moor 76, 120, 122 (ill)
Belsize estate 11 (map), 13, 15, 80
Belsize House 15, 16, 18, 20 (ill), 20 (map), 24, 26, 34, 35, 47, 80
Belsize Lane 16
Belsize Park Gardens 111
Belsize School 116
Belsize Village 80
Benefit Societies 55
Bennett, T.P. 126, 131
Bernstein, Sidney 127
Besant, Annie 109
Bevan, Robert 112
Bianchi, Mr 68
Binning, Lady 143
Bird-in-Hand 95
Births in Hampstead 19
Black Boy and Still 127
Black Lion, Kilburn 23
Black Lion, West End 22
Blacketts Well 17
Blake, William 108
Blakette, Richard 17
Bleak Hall 44
Bleamire, William 55
Blue Star Garage and site 22, 138
Boden, William 26
Bodkin, William 60
Bolton House, Windmill Hill 106
Boydell, Josiah 59–61, 62 (ill), 106
Brabazon see Le Brabazon
Brain, Dennis 68

Branch Hill 17
Branch Hill Lodge 44, 90, 138–9, 139 (ill)
Brawne, Fanny 107
Brewery, South End Green 51
Brewhouse 23 (cf Hampstead Brewery)
Brickfields 18, 74
Brooke, Sir Henry 137, 141
Brown, Charles Armitage 107
Buckingham Duke of 25
Buckland Crescent 80, 116 (No. 18)
Bull and Bush 22, 51, 53, 102
Burdett-Coutts, Baroness Angela 75
Burgess, Henry Weech 86
Burgess Park 86
Burgh House 31, 32 (ill), 37, 60, 61 (ill), 127, 143
Burgh House Trust 143
Burial Ground – see Hampstead, burial ground
Burney, Fanny 37
Burrell, Sir Charles 71
Buses 95, 97, 98 (ill)

Camden Arts Centre 142
Camden History Society 8, 143
Camden, London Borough of 141
Campaign for Nuclear Disarmament 135
Campden Charity 38
Campden, Lady 38
Canfield Gardens 85
Cannon, Charles 86
Cannon Hall 37, 42, 108
Carlile, Edward 51
Carlile House and estate 25, 39, 51, 90, 91 (ill)
Carline, Richard 112, 143
Carlingford Road 90
Cart and Horses 22
Caston, Robert 36
Caswell Eagle 57
Cedar Lawn, North End Way 120
Central School of Speech and Drama 130
Chalcots estate – see Eton College estate
Charities 38
Charlton House, Greenwich 16
Charter AD986 9, 12 (ill)
Chesterfield, Earl of 80
Chicken House 25, 26 (ill), 84 (ill), 90
Child, Robert 17
Childs Hill 17, 38
Childs Hill House 86
Cholmeley, Sir Roger 27
Christ Church 42, 57, 58–9
Christian, Ewan 58
Church Row 47 (No 18), 108 (No 26)
Churchyard – see Hampstead, burial ground
Cinemas 131
Circle 111
Clapp, Peter 143
Clarke, Sir Thomas 44
Classic cinema 131
Clausen, George 110
Cloth Hill 18
Cock and Hoop 47, 48 (ill)
Coenen, William 127
Cold Bath Pond 30
Coleman, William 51
Collins, Wilkie 108
Collins, William 108
Combrune Michael 51
Commons Preservation Society 74
Compayne Gardens 85
Constable, John 61, 107, 107 (ill), 116
Constables 36, 37
Constantine Road 93
Cotton, Colonel Percy 88
Coward, Noel 130

Cressy Road 93, 95
Crimes 26
Crocketts Court 66
Crosfield, Sir Arthur 76
Crossfield Road 116
Crump, Mrs 93
Culverhouse, John 78
Curry, James 51

Davidson, Henry 80
Dawkes 58
Deane, William 26
Deaths in Hampstead 19
Deormod's Wick 9
Dilke, Charles Wentworth 107
Dinerman, Davison and Partners 143
Dingley, Charles 53, 76
Dispensary 55
Domesday Survey 9, 15
Downshire Hill 51, 51 (ill), 52, 112 (No. 21), 112 (No. 47), 141, 143 (No. 49a)
Downside Crescent 80
Drazin 143
Drill Hall, Holly Bush Vale 60, 130
Drinking fountain, South End Green 93
Duff, Peggy 135
Duffield, John 30–1
du Maurier, Daphne 108
du Maurier, George 108, 109 (ill)
du Maurier, Sir Gerald 108
Duncan, Rev. J. 116

East and West India Dock, Birmingham Junction Railway – see North London Railway
East Heath Road 31, 42, 57, 120, 82 (Nos. 17–20)
East Middlesex Militia 60, 60 (ill)
East Park estate 15, 72–5, 83
Edmonton Union 64
Education – see Schools
El Serranos 134
Eldon Grove 111
Eldorado cinema 131
Electricity Department and depot 113, 114 (ill)
Ellerdale Road 82, 116, 109 (No. 6)
Ellis Clough Williams 62, 120
Ellis Havelock 120
Elms, The 23
Embassy Theatre 127
Empson, William 143
Erskine, Thomas 46
Erskine House 46, 92 (ill)
Ethelred the Unready 9
Eton College estate 10 (map), 12, 53, 79, 80, 136
Evans, B.B. 126
Everyman Cinema 60
Everyman Theatre 130
Eyre estate 52, 79

Fabian Society 117
Fairfax-Jones, Jim and Tess 130
Fairground, Vale of Health 131
Farmer, Alan 8
Fenton, Philip 44
Fenton House 43 (ill), 44, 143
Fiennes, Celia 29
Finchley Road 16, 48–9, 71, 91 (ill), 97 (ill), 126, 131
Finchley Road station 98, 99 (ill)
Finsberg, Geoffrey 142
Fire stations 70
Firs, The 46, 89 (ill)
Fitzjohn's Avenue 16, 83 (ill), 85, 86, 109 (No. 6), 86 (No. 55), 109 (No 61)
Flask, The 22
Flask Walk 37, 61 (No. 65), 129 (ill)

Fleet river 15, 47, 51, 80
Fleet Road 66, 95
Flitcroft, Henry 38, 39, 44, 46, 57, 106
Foley House 31
Forster's 126
Forsyth, Thomas 80
Fortune Green 17, 68, 78
Fowle, Mr 78
Fowler's 126
Freemasons Arms 52
Freud, Anna 110
Freud, E.L. 124
Freud, Sigmund 109
Friends Meeting House 57, 59 (ill)
Frognal 17, 37, 44, 46, 47, 90, 109 (No. 39), 111 (No. 66), 46 (No. 94), 46, 57, 110 (Nos. 103–9), 46 (Nos. 108–110)
Frognal Bijou Picture Palace 131
Frognal Close 124
Frognal Lane 16
Frognal Priory 92 (ill), 124
Frognal Way 111 (No. 9)
Fry, Maxwell 111

Gabo, Naum 111
Gainsborough, Earl of 29
Gainsborough Gardens 30
Gardnor Mansions 120
Gas supplies 63
Gattaker, Thomas 46
Gay, Bernard 142
Gayton Road 22, 30
Gaze, G.H. 126
George, The 22
Gertler, Mark 111
Gibb, Thomas Eccleston 93
Gibbet, North End Way 26
Gipsies 76 (ill), 78
Glendyne, Lord 138
Golders Hill estate 76
Goldinger, Erno 112
Goldhurst Terrace 85
Goss, Arthur 132, 135
Goss, S. 132
Gowan, James 143
Grange, The 90
Gray, Frederick 131
Great Canfield, Essex 16
Green Man 30
Greenaway, Kate 68, 109
Greencroft Gardens 85
Greenhill estate 82
Greenhill flats 82, 120
Great Plague 19
Great Tree, The 22
Greville Place 52
Grigson, Geoffrey 111
Gropius, Walter 112
Grove Lodge 44
Grylls, Thomas 127

Haberdashers' Aske School 116
Hales, Prof. John W. 9
Hall Oak Farm 16
Hall School 116
Hampfield, George 44
Hampstead –
  Borough Council 90, 113, 117, 136–8, 141–3
  Burial ground 17
  Cemetery 68, 69 (ill)
  Country houses 17–19, 24
  Incorporation into London 62
  Manor 9–16
  Manor house 16, 18 (map)
  Parish registers 19
  Population 12, 19
  Vestry 36, 37, 55, 62, 64, 113
  Vestry/Town Hall 68, 69 (ill), 70, 137
Hampstead and Highgate Express 59, 66, 131, 135, 138, 142
Hampstead Antiquarian and Historical Society 127
Hampstead Artists' Council 142–3

Hampstead Brewery 22–3, 30, 126, 126 (ill)
Hampstead Choral Society 127
Hampstead Comprehensive School 116
Hampstead Conservative Association 117, 135, 141
Hampstead Conservatoire 127, 128 (ill)
Hampstead Constitutional Club 62
Hampstead Dinner Club 61
Hampstead Dispensary 56 (ill)
Hampstead Garden Suburb 78
Hampstead General Hospital 66
Hampstead Green 49, 66, 108
Hampstead Grove 44
Hampstead Heath 15, 21 (map), 71–4
Hampstead Heath Extension 77–8
Hampstead Heath Protection Society – see Heath and Old Hampstead Society
Hampstead High Street 22 (No. 14), 16 (No. 28), 22 (No. 31), 61, 63 (ill), 82 (Nos. 85–8)
Hampstead Hill Gardens 110
Hampstead Historic Club 120
Hampstead Junction Railway 82, 88, 98
Hampstead Labour Party 117, 135–6, 141
Hampstead Liberals 117
Hampstead Loyal Volunteers 59–60
Hampstead News 68
Hampstead Parliamentary Debating Society 127
Hampstead Parochial Benefit Society 55
Hampstead Parochial School 56–7
Hampstead Picture Palace 131
Hampstead Provident Dispensary 55
Hampstead Ponds 47
Hampstead Scientific Society 127
Hampstead Square 42, 58
Hampstead Subscription Library 61, 63 (ill)
Hampstead Theatre Club 137 (ill), 138
Hampstead Water Company 47, 93
Hampstead Wells 29–33, 30 (map)
Harben, Sir Henry 113, 114 (ill)
Hare and Hounds 53, 131 (ill), 132
Harvey, James 57
Hatch, Samuel 53
Hatches Bottom 53
Haverstock Hill 17
Haverstock Lodge 80
Head Nightingale 26
Hearth Tax 24–5
Heartfield, John 112
Heath and Old Hampstead Society (incorporating predecessors) 102, 127, 143
Heath End House 77, 44 (ill), 46
Heath Mount School 116, 93 (ill)
Heath Street 17, 37, 57, 116, 121 (ill), 143, 131 (No. 64)
Heathfield 57
Heathlands 45 (ill), 46
Hendon 9, 12
Henley House School 116
Hepworth, Barbara 110
Hereford House, South End Green 93, 131
High Hill Bookshop 134
High Hill Press 8
Hill, Octavia 75
Hill, Sir Rowland 66, 108, 109 (ill)
Hill, The 45 (ill), 46
Hillfield, Haverstock Hill 68
Hoare, John Gurney 46, 73, 75 (ill)
Hoare, Samuel jnr 46
Hoare, Samuel snr 46
Holford, Charles 42, 60–1
Holl, Frank 109
Hollow Elm 27, 27 (ill), 29
Holly Bush Hill 62
Holly Bush Tavern 62
Holly Bush Vale 57, 130
Holly Hill 18
Holly Hill House 25
Holly Mount 57, 66
Holly Place 66
Honywood, Benoni 16
Honywood, Isaac 25, 39
Hopkins, Michael 143
Hornsey 9
Hornsey Journal 68

Horse buses 22, 95, 97
Hospital of St James 12
Hospital of St John of Jerusalem 13
Howard, Fulke Greville 52
Howell, Mr 35
Howitt Road 110
Hunt, Joan 27–8
Hunt, Leigh 54, 107, 107 (ill)

Ice house, Gainsborough Gardens 30
Ikin, Christopher 8
Imperial Gas Company 63
Inner London Motorway 139
Inns 22
Inverforth, Lord 46
Inverforth House 46
Isaaman, Gerald 142
Isokon and Isokon flats 111, 140 (ill)
Iveagh, 1st Earl 77
Ivy Bank 82
Ivy House 124

Jack Straw's Castle 38, 41, 46, 53, 88 (ill), 102, 130 (ill)
Jackson, Jeannette 142
James I 25
Jealous George Samuel 66
John Barnes 124, 126
John de Neuport 17
John Street 51
Johnson, Lancelott 27
Johnson, Samuel 31, 42, 44
Jones, Sheila 135
Jubilee line 99

Keats, John 106–7, 106 (ill)
Keats Grove 51
Keats House 121 (ill), 124
Kemplay Road 90
Kendall, H.E. 70
Kenwood estate 16, 47, 53, 76–7
Kidderpore Hall 86 (ill), 86
Kilburn Empire 130
Kilburn High Road 126
Kilburn Palace 130
Kilburn Priory estate 10 (map), 12–13, 15 (ill), 47, 52, 90
Kilburn Priory (road) 90
Kilburn Times 68
Kilburn Town Hall 130
Kilburn Wells 36, 36 (ill)
King Alfred's School 116
King Henry's Road 111, 136
King of Bohemia 22, 23 (ill)
King William IV (public house) 22
Kings Arms 22, 70
Kings Head 22
Kingscroft Road 90
Kingsgate 90
Kingswell 17, 143
Kit-Cat Club 41, 42
Knight, Charles 61
Knights Templars 13
Knowles-Brown 126
Kokoschka, Oskar 111

Ladywell Court, East Heath Road 42, 57
Lancaster Grove 70
Lane, Joseph 125 (ill)
Langtry, Lillie 109
Lauderdale House, Highgate 24
Lavie, Germain 80
Lawn Road 66, 80
Lawrence, D.H. 103
Le Brabazon, Sir Roger 15, 17
Leg of Mutton Pond 56
Legg, Henry 66
Leighton House, Alexandra Road 109
Leverhulme, Lord (William Lever) 46, 124
Levy, Ted, Benjamin and Partners 143
Libraries – see Hampstead Subscription Library and Public Libraries
Lighting and Watching 37

Linnel' John 53, 107, 108
Linton, James 110
Lister, Lord 68
Lithos Road 113
Littleworth 46
Lloyd, Marie 68
Load of Hay 22
Logs, The, East Heath Road 82 (ill)
London government 63–4
London County Council 77–8, 95
London North Western Railway 79, 98
London School Board 116, 124
Long Room (1st) 30–1, 39
Long Room (2nd) 31, 32 (ill), 33 (ill), 33, 62
Longman, Thomas Norton and family 60, 61, 82
Lord, Dr Charles 64
Lower Purloins 16
Lucas, Colin 111
Lund, William 80
Lyndhurst Road Congregational church 58

McBeth, Robert 110
MacDermott, Norman 130
MacDonald, Ramsay 110
Mall Studios 110
Manor House – see Hampstead, manor house
Mansfield, 4th Earl 74
Mansion flats 120
Marriages in Hampstead 19
MARS 111
Marsh, Richard 52
Maryon Mews 140 (ill), 143
Maryon Wilson estate 14 (map), 15–16, 71–4, 79
Maryon Wilson, Sir John M. 74
Maryon Wilson, Spencer 86
Maryon Wilson, Sir Thomas jnr 49, 55, 58–9, 71–4, 72 (ill), 80, 83–6
Maryon Wilson, Sir Thomas snr 48
Mayle, Sidney 127
Maynard, Constance 118
Medical Officer of Health 64
Medical Research Council 25
Melville, Sir James Cosmo 42
Metropolitan and St John's Wood Railway 82, 99
Metropolitan Asylums Board 66
Metropolitan Board of Works 64, 74, 75
Metropolitan Fire Brigade 70
Metropolitan Police 37, 68
Mew, Frederick 70
Midland Railway 88, 99
Mill houses 23
Milligan, Robert 49
Milne, A.A. 116
Milne, J.V. 116
Mitchell, Arnold 117
Mitchell, Thomas 57
Mondrian, Piet 111
Montagu, Edward 57
Moore, Henry 110
Morel, Abbe 57
Moreland Hall 109, 138
Morley, Prof. Henry 113
Mortimer Crescent 116
Mortimer Road 90
Mother Huff's 23
Motorway Box 139
Mott, Alfred 70
Mount, The 44, 106
Munich, C.J. 127
Municipal Electors Association 135
Murray, John 61
Music 127

Nags Head 22, 51
Nash, Paul 111, 112
Nassington Road 93
National Schools 57
Neave, Sir Thomas 90
Netherwood Street 136
New College 79, 120
New End 19, 27, 29, 38, 57
New End Hospital 38
New Georgia 36

New Grove House 44
New River Company 29, 37, 62–3
Newton, E.E. 8
Nicholson, Ben 110
Nihill, Lucy 57
Norrie, Ian 134
North Captain Fountain 44
North End 9, 19, 52–3
North End Place 53
North End Road 116
North London Railway 80, 98
North West Fever Hospital 66
Northcliffe, Lord 66, 108, 116
Northern Heights Footpath Association 127
Northern Line 77–8, 100 (ill), 102
Norway House 33, 34 (ill), 35 (ill), 124
Norway Yard 95

Oak Hill Park 90
Oak Lodge 90
Observatory 127, 128 (ill)
Odeon cinemas 131
Old Brewery Mews 143
Old Grove House 44
O'Neill, Daniel 24
Open Air Art Exhibition 143
Oriel House 57
Orwell, George 111
Osborne, Lord Sidney Godolphin 108
Osborne, Thomas 33–4
Ostend House 44
Overseers of the Poor 37

Palgrave, Sir Francis 66, 108
Palmer, Charles 80
Palmer, Samuel 108
Palmerston Road 136
Parish church 16, 17, 19 (ill), 38–9, 39 (ill), 58–9
Parish priest – see Vicars
Park, John James 47
Park Dwellings 117
Parkgate 39, 46
Parkhill Road 80, 110, 136, 111 (No. 60)
Parkhurst, John 131–2
Parliament Hill (road) 93
Parliament Hill Fields 16, 74, 75
Paterson, William 47
Pavlova Anna 124
Penn Studio 111
Penrose, Sir Roland 112
Pepys, Samuel 34
Perceval, Spencer 80
Perceval Avenue 82
Perrins Court 59, 131
Peters, Mrs 90
Pevrel, Ranulf 15
Pevsner, Nikolaus 70
Philanthropy 55–7
Philo-Investigists 56–7
Pickett's Farm 93, 117
Pilgrim, James 38
Pitt, Dr David 135
Pitt, William, the elder 53
Pitt House 53, 133
Platt, Thomas Pell 86
Platts Lane 90 (ill)
Playhouse 31
Playhouse cinema 131
Pocock, George 52
Pocock, John Thomas 52
Poliakoff, Vladimir 132
Police stations 68
Politics in Hampstead 110, 117, 134–6, 138–9, 141–2
Pond Street 19, 22, 49, 51
Poor Houses 38, 53
Poor relief 26
Pope Alexander 31
Poulter, James 60
Pound 53
Povey, Charles 34–5
Presbyterians in Hampstead 39, 59
Primrose Hill 9

Primrose Hill Station 80
Prince Arthur Road 85
Priory Lodge 44
Priory Road 83
Pritchard, Jack 111
Prospect Place 17
Pryors, The 43 (ill), 44, 120
Public Houses 22
Public Libraries 79, 113, 124, 132 (ill), 133, 136 (ill), 137

Queen Mary Maternity Home 124

Railways 82–3, 88, 90, 98–102
Ratepayers' Association 134
Rayne, Max 136, 138
Raynes, John 26
Read, Herbert 112
Red Lion, Kilburn 23
Red Lion, Rosslyn Hill 26, 68
Reservoirs 37, 86
Rhodes, Thomas 83
Rhys, Ernest 120, 127
Rivers 47
Robert of Kingswell 17
Roberts, Thomas 22, 80
Rogues and Felons Society 37
Romney, George 44, 105 (ill), 106
Romney's House 62, 105 (ill), 106, 120
Rondu Road 90
Rookery, Greenhill 81 (ill), 82
Room, Leslie 137, 142
Roose-Evans, James 137 (ill), 138
Rosecroft Avenue 86
Rosslyn, Earl of (Alexander Wedderburn) 44, 80
Rosslyn Hill Chapel 39, 40 (ill), 51, 59, 103
Rosslyn Hill Park 80
Rosslyn House 49, 80, 81 (ill)
Rosslyn Lodge 57, 120
Rothermere, Lord 109
Rous, Joseph 31
Rowntree, Fred 57
Royal Free Hospital 66, 138
Royal Soldiers Daughters Home 82, 142 (ill)
Rudall Crescent 90
Rumsey, Thomas 38, 51
Ruskin, John 109
Russell, Mrs 116

Sadlers Wells 29
St Columba's Hospital 137
St Dunstan's School for the Blind 137
St Johns parish church – see Parish church
St John's, Downshire Hill 51–2, 68
St John's Park estate 79, 80
St Mary's parish church – see Parish church
St Mary's, Holly Place 17, 57, 58 (ill)
St Pancras parish and vestry 9, 37
St Stephen's 49, 68, 108
Salter, Joseph 93
Sandgate 9
Sandy Heath 9, 53
Saunderson, John 39, 46
Schools 27, 116
Schreiber, Chaim 143
Schreiner, Olive 120
Scott, George Gilbert the ygr 58, 108
Scott, Sir George Gilbert the elder 108
Scott, Sir Walter 106
Searle, C.G. 57
Sedley, Sir Charles 104
Sexton 37
Sharp, Cecil 127
Shaw, George Bernard 120
Shaw, R. Norman 109
Shaw, Roy 135
Shaw-Lefevre, Sir George 74
Shepherd's Path 49
Shepherd's Walk 49
Shepherd's Well 47, 49, 50 (ill)
Shoot-up Hill estate 11 (map), 13, 17, 88, 90
Shoot-up Hill Farm 90

159

Shops 23, 85–6, 124–6
Sickert, Walter 110
Silverman, Sidney 135
Sion Chapel 34
Skardu Road 90
Skeaping, John 110
Slanning, John 53
Smalley, Conrad 61
Smallpox Hospital 66, 67 (ill)
Soup Kitchen 55
South End Close 117
South End Green 50 (ill), 51, 93, 95, 131
South Hampstead Advertiser 68
South Hampstead High School 115 (ill), 116
South Hill Park 93
Spaniards Road 22
Sparkes, Michael 29
Spence, Basil 137
Spencer, Stanley 112
Spender, Stephen 111
Squire, Joshua 42
Squire's Mount 42 (ill), 44
Stage coaches 95
Stanfield House – see Hampstead High Street (Nos. 85–8)
Steele, Sir Richard 41, 104 (ill), 104
Steele's Cottage 41, 104
Steevens, George 42
Stephenson, Cecil 110
Stephenson, Robert 108
Stock, John 38
Stocks 37, 38 (ill)
Streatham Wells 29
Streatley Place 96 (ill)
Suffragettes 117
Sun House, Frognal Way 111
Sunday school 56
Survey 1312 17
Surveyors of the Highways 37
Swiss Cottage 68, 79, 82, 135 (ill), 137, 138
Swiss Cottage Skating Rink 66

Tanza Road 93
Taverns 22
Tensleys 66
Teulon, Samuel S. 68, 108
Teil, John 86
Thompson, Prof. F.M.L. 8, 18
Thompson, John 124
Thrale, Mrs. 31
Three Horseshoes 22
Three Tuns 22, 126
Tile making 23, 24
Tonson, Jacob 42
Town Hall – see Hampstead, Vestry/Town Hall
Town Improvements 85
Trams 95–7
Trinity Chapel, Rosslyn Hill 59
Turner, John 46
Tyburn river 47

Uhlman, Fred and Diana 112
Underground railways 99, 100 (ill), 102
Unitarians 59, 61
University College School 25, 47, 116–7
Upper Flask/Upper Heath 26, 40 (ill), 41, 42, 124
Upper Park Road 80
Upper Purloins 16
Upton, Col. Arthur 90

Vale of Health 9, 38, 47, 53–4, 53 (ill), 107
Vale of Health Hotel 112
Vane, Sir Henry 25
Vane House 25, 25 (ill), 82, 142 (ill)
Vestry Clerk 37
Vestry Hall – see Hampstead, Vestry/Town Hall
Vicarage 16
Vicars 17
Victoria Tea Gardens 58
Vincent John 30, 126
Vine House 42

Vizard, P.E. 127
Volunteers 59–60

Waad, Sir William 26, 27
Wade, Christopher 8
War memorial 130 (ill)
Wartime 120, 132–3
Watch House 37, 38 (ill)
Watching 37
Watchmen 36
Water supplies 49, cf Shepherd's Well
Waterhouse, Alfred 57
Watling Street 9
Waugh, Evelyn 116
Weatherall House 32 (ill)
Webb, Sidney 120
Wedderburn, Alexander – see Earl of Rosslyn
Well Road 29, 30
Well Walk 9, 31, 109
Well Walk Chapel 31, 39, 58, 59, 60
Wells, H.G. 116
Wells, Sir Spencer 76
Wells Charity 38
Wells and Campden Charity 66
Wells Buildings 85
Wells Coates 111
Wells House 31
Wells House (local authority) 136
Wells Tavern 30, 107
Wentworth Place 107
West End 19, 52, 86, 88, 87 (map)
West End Fair 52
West End Green 52, 78
West End Lane 16, 47, 97 (ill), 136

West Heath Road 143
West Middlesex Water Company 86
Westbourne river 47, 117
Westcroft estate 117
Westfield College 117
Westminster, Abbey of 9, 16, 18
Westminster, Dean and Chapter 80
Westrope's bookshop 111
Whitaker, Ben 141
White, Henry 52
White Hart 22, 127
White Horse 22, 51
Whitestone Pond 122 (ill)
Wildwood 53
Wilkie, Sir David 106
Willes, Sir Francis 46
Willesden 9
Willoughby, Dobson 60
Willoughby Road 90
Willow Road 52, 60, 112
Wilson, Charlotte 117
Windmills 23, 24 (ill)
Witchcraft 27–8
Wodewarde, Walter 17
Woods William 51
Workhouse 25, 37, 38, 55, 64, 85 (ill)
Wotton, Lord 34
Wyatt, Sir William 66
Wyldes House and estate 12, 53, 78, 108, 117, 118 (ill)

Yerkes, Charles Tyson 102
Yorkshire Grey Yard 115 (ill)